DICTIONARY
OF MARKS ~
POTTERY
AND
PORCELAIN

by
Ralph M. and Terry H. Kovel

CROWN PUBLISHERS, INC.　•　NEW YORK

TO RIX AND DOROTHY

OUR MOTHERS

Library of Congress Catalog Card Number: 53-5247

ISBN: 0-517-001411

Printed in the United States of America

Twenty-sixth Printing, November, 1975

CONTENTS

FOREWORD

Every collector knows that the least reliable but the quickest way to identify a piece of porcelain is to identify the mark. This book was written to make this identification easier. We warn the reader that marks are often forged and changed and that this book does not attempt to tell you that all porcelain marked in a certain way came from a certain factory. We give you a listing of the better-known marks and enough information so that you can learn more about your porcelains, if you wish to do so. Research and experience will tell you if the color, texture, weight, design, or general "feel" of the piece is right. This book will help you identify the mark. It is quite different from any other book of marks that the reader may have seen and, therefore, in order to use it properly it is necessary to explain the actual layout of the pages.

The book is divided into two parts. We have arranged the marks according to their shapes. The first half contains those marks that look like letters or words. Often a mark may resemble a C or a crescent or some other letter or shape. There are subheadings for each section suggesting other parts of the book that may contain the mark you seek. The second half of the book contains marks that look like a circle, square, bird or animal shape, etc. The Contents and the Index of Marks give the complete listing of these sections; the Index of Marks also gives additional cross references, such as specific animals, associated shapes, etc.

We have tried to put the simple shapes at the beginning of the book. For example, if your mark is the picture of an anchor with an A beneath it, look under Section A. A would be the easiest part of the mark to recognize. If the mark is a circle with a bird and writing inside, look under Section Circle and Sign. (Marks will often be blurred and sometimes it is impossible to read the writing, so we have, whenever possible, listed the mark by its outer outline.) If you cannot find the mark in that particular Section, look through the Index of Marks, for there you will find a complete listing of all marks that contain birds, regardless of the outer shape.

The explanation of each mark listed in this book is as follows:

(1) The first word, that in capitals, is the name of the city in which the factory is located. If the city is not known then the country is listed in capital letters.

(2) The next word is, if not already given, the name of the country.

(3) The factory name or the name of some person intimately connected with the factory, such as the founder or the most famous potter or artist, is the next part of the explanation.

(4) The type of ware is listed next, if it is known.

(5) The method of producing the mark on the object is described next.

(6) The color of the mark is next.

(7) The date when the mark was used is at the end of the description.

Often only part of this information is available. For example, the first mark listed in the book is as follows: (1) ALCORA, city; (2) *Spain,* country; (3) unknown; (4) *Porcelain,* type of ware; (5) *Incised,* how the mark is produced; (6) *Red, gold, black,* color of mark; (7) *From 1784,* date when the mark was used. This system will become clear to the reader quite quickly.

We have tried to make this book as complete as possible but naturally some marks will not be listed. The marks chosen to be included are those we felt would be seen most often by the average collector. Many American marks and twentieth century marks are included but very few are listed from the sixteenth century or earlier. No majolica has been discussed in this book because that is a separate problem in identification for the collector. No Chinese or Japanese marks are included because our new method of classification would add nothing in this field. If you wish to find out about these marks we suggest you read *The Book of Pottery and Porcelain,* by Warren E. Cox, or *Marks and Monograms on European and Oriental Pottery and Porcelain,* by William Chaffers.

There is some confusion in any reference book containing Delft marks. The Delft factories had a special way of registering their marks and the factory names which were registered are often misspelled. In this book each factory name is written in Dutch and then translated into English, so the reader will be able to find these names in other source books. Because each writer spells these names a little differently and each century saw a change in the actual way the Dutch language was written, we have written each name in its modern-day Dutch spelling. Do not be upset if this spelling is different from the one you are accustomed to using. Often, for the Delft factory, you may find a person's name listed instead of a factory name. This is usually an artist or the factory owner and is also important for further research.

There are two important marks that need separate explanations to the reader. The first is the Sevres mark, which can be found under Section Lines. For the accurate date of this mark consult the following table:

A	— 1753	X	— 1775	XI	— 1803		
B	— 1754	Y	— 1776	≑	— 1804		
C	— 1755	Z	— 1777	�介	— 1805		
D	— 1756	AA	— 1778	⽂	— 1806		
E	— 1757	BB	— 1779	7	— 1807		
F	— 1758	CC	— 1780	8	— 1808		
G	— 1759	DD	— 1781	9	— 1809		
H	— 1760	EE	— 1782	10	— 1810		
I	— 1761	FF	— 1783	o.z. (onze)	— 1811		
J	— 1762	GG	— 1784	d.z. (douze)	— 1812		
K	— 1763	HH	— 1785	t.z. (treize)	— 1813		
L	— 1764	II	— 1786	q.z. (quatorze)	1814		
M	— 1765	JJ	— 1787	q.n. (quinze)	— 1815		
N	— 1766	KK	— 1788	s.z. (seize)	— 1816		
O	— 1767	LL	— 1789	d.s. (diz sept)	1817		
P	— 1768	MM	— 1790				
Q	— 1769	NN	— 1791				
R	— 1770	OO	— 1792	After 1817 the year is shown by the last two figures only:			
S	— 1771	PP	— 1793				
T	— 1772	To July 17		18 — 1818			
U	— 1773	Tg	— 1801	19 — 1819			
V	— 1774	X	— 1802	etc.			

The other mark is that used in England from 1842 to 1883. To understand this mark completely, notice the tables below. This mark was often used with other marks that designated the factory or pattern name.

Mark A

The mark above (A) was used from 1842 to 1867. The Roman numerals in the circle at the top of the mark indicate the type of ware manufactured.

Table 1

I — metal	III — glass
II — wood	IV — earthenware

The letter below this circle tells the year of manufacture, as follows:

Table 2

X — 1842	P — 1851	Z — 1860
H — 1843	D — 1852	R — 1861
C — 1844	Y — 1853	O — 1862
A — 1845	J — 1854	G — 1863
I — 1846	E — 1855	N — 1864
F — 1847	L — 1856	W — 1865
U — 1848	K — 1857	Q — 1866
S — 1849	B — 1858	T — 1867
V — 1850	M — 1859	

The letter in the left-hand corner of the diamond-shaped mark (A) indicates the month of the year in which the object was manufactured.

Table 3

C — January	E — May	D — September
G — February	M — June	B — October
W — March	I — July	K — November
H — April	R — August	A — December

The number in the right-hand corner of the diamond indicates the day of the month in which the object was manufactured. The number in the bottom corner of the mark tells the manufacturer of the object.

The mark below (B) was used from 1868 to 1883.

Mark B

The Roman numerals in the circle at the top of the mark indicate the type of ware manufactured, as it did in the other diamond-shaped mark (see *Table 1*). The number in the circle below the Roman numeral indicates the day of the month. The letter in the lower corner of the diamond-shaped mark (B) indicates the month of the year in which the object was manufactured. The same table of letters applies to this mark (B) as to the other mark (A) (*see Table 3*). The number in the left-hand corner tells the manufacturer of the object. The letter in the right-hand corner indicates the year of manufacture, as follows:

Table 4

X	—	1868	U	—	1874	Y — 1879
H	—	1869	S	—	1875	J — 1880
C	—	1870	V	—	1876	E — 1881
A	—	1871	P	—	1877	L — 1882
I	—	1872	D	—	1878	K — 1883
F	—	1873				

RALPH M. KOVEL

TERRY H. KOVEL

BIBLIOGRAPHY

The following is a list of books that we would like to recommend to the reader who wishes to learn more about pottery and porcelain:

Marks and Monograms on European and Oriental Pottery and Porcelain, by William Chaffers
The Book of Pottery and Porcelain, by Warren E. Cox
The Practical Book of Chinaware, by Everlein and Ramsdell
Pottery and Porcelain, by Frederick Litchfield
American Potters and Pottery, by John Ramsay
Early American Pottery and China, by John Spargo

a   b   c   d   e   f

SECTION A
See also Sections
H, Lines

(a) ALCORA, Spain. Porcelain. Incised red, gold, black. From 1784.
(b) PARIS, France. Hard paste. Painted red, gold. From 1793.
(c) BOW, Great Britain. Porcelain. 1744-1776. (d) BOW, Great
Britain. Porcelain. 1740-1775. (e) BOW, Great Britain. Porcelain.
Circa 1744. (f) HOLLAND. Oude Amstel. Porcelain. 1782.

g   h   i   j   k   l

(g) ST. AMAND-LES-EAUX, France. Fayence. Est. 1740. (h)
HOLLAND. Arnheim. Fayence. 1780. (i) HOLLAND. Oude Amstel. Porcelain. 1784-1800. (j) KIEL, Germany. Fayence. Circa 1770.
(k) ALCORA, Spain. Porcelain. Painted or incised red, gold, black.
From 1784. (l) PARIS, France. Hard paste. Painted red. 1770-1780.

m   n   o   p   q   r

(m) ANSBACH, Germany. Porcelain. Est. 1758. (n) BOW, Great
Britain. Porcelain. 1740-1775. (o) BOW, Great Britain. Porcelain.
1744-1776. (p) PARIS, France. Sometimes with a crown. 1775-1869.
(q) PARIS, France. Hard paste. Painted red. Est. 1778. (r) ST.
CLOUD, France. Porcelain. 1670-1773.

a   b   c   d   e

(a) PARIS, France. Hard paste. Painted. 1773. (b) ALCORA,
Spain. Porcelain. Painted red, gold, or black; or incised. From 1784.
(c) PERSIA, TURKEY, SYRIA. Fayence. 19th century. (d) CO-
PENHAGEN, Denmark. Fayence. Mark under glaze. 1903. (e)
WEDGWOOD, Great Britain. Mark of a painter, Thomas Allen.
1875-1905.

f   g   h   i   j   k

(f) HOLLAND. Weesp. 1764-1771. (g) ANSBACH, Germany. Porcelain. Circa 1759. (h) BRISTOL, Great Britain. Pottery and porcelain. Blue, or gold overglaze. 18th century. (i) ROTTERDAM, Holland. A. Luffen, artist. Fayence. 1700. (j) HOLLAND. De Griekse
A (The Greek A). Fayence. 1765. (k) MOUSTIERS, France. Joseph Olery. Fayence. 18th century.

l   m   n   o   p

(l) MOUSTIERS, France. Joseph Olery. Fayence. 18th century.
(m) NYMPHENBERG, Germany. Porcelain. Impressed or incised.
Est. 1747. (n) BORDEAUX, France. Est. circa 1783. (o) St.
AMAND-LES-EAUX, France. Soft paste. Est. 1800. (p) SEVRES,
France. Soft paste. Painted blue. 1753. (Often copied.)

a   b   c   d   e   f

(a) SEVRES, France. Soft or hard paste. 1777-1778. (b)
FRANCE. Painted red. 18th century. (c) ARRAS, France. Hard
paste. Est. 1782. (d) ANSBACH, Bavaria. Hard Paste. Painted blue.
Early 18th century. (e) LILLE, France. Fayence. Painted. 18th century. (f) MOUSTIERS, France. Fayence. 18th century.

g   h   i   j

(g) ITALY. Porcelain. 1752. (h) FONTAINEBLEAU, France. Fayence. 17th century. (i) ITALY. Porcelain. 1752. (j) MOUSTIERS,
France. Fayence. 18th century.

k   l   m   n   o   p

(k) BURTON-ON-TRENT, Great Britain. Ashby Potter's Guild.
Pottery. Est. 1909. (l) DAEHMEL, Germany. Est. 1854. (m)
PARIS, France. Advenir Lamarre. Hard paste. Painted 1773. (n)
AMSTERDAM (Amstel), Holland. Daeuber, director. Hard paste.
Painted blue. 1783. (o) PARIS, France. Gros Caillou. 1773. (p)
HOLLAND. Delft. Painted blue. 1774.

a   b   c   d   e   f

(a) ANDENNES, France. Pottery. Impressed. Early 19th century. (b) LIMOGES, France. 1842-1898. (c) SWITZERLAND. Fayence. 1689. (d) BOW, Great Britain. Porcelain. 1744-1776. (e) ROR-STAND, Sweden. Fayence. Est. 1727. (f) RORSTAND, Sweden. Fayence. From 1758.

g   h   i   j   k

(g) TOULOUSE, France. Fouqué-Arnoux and Company. Fayence. Painted. 1820. (h) SAVONA, Italy. Pottery. 17th century. (i) ROCKHILL, Pennsylvania, U.S.A. Charles Headman. 1840-1870. (j) BRISTOL, Great Britain. 1703-1803. (k) HOLLAND. De Griekse A (The Greek A). Fayence. 1765.

l   m   n   o   p   q

(l) HOLLAND. De Griekse A (The Greek A). Fayence. 1765. (m) BOW, Great Britain. Porcelain. 1744-1776. (n) HOLLAND. De Griekse A (The Greek A). Fayence. 1759. (o) HOLLAND. De Griekse Å (The Greek A). Fayence. Painted blue. 1764. (p) HOL-LAND. De Ster (The Star). A Kiell, artist. Delft. 1764. (q) HOL-LAND. De Witte Ster (The White Star). A. Kiell, artist. Delft. Painted blue. 1764.

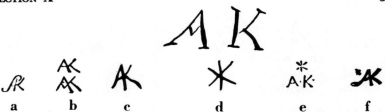

a   b   c   d   e   f

(a) HOLLAND. Samuel Piet Roerder, artist. Delft. Painted. 1650.
(b) HOLLAND. De Witte Ster (The White Star). A Kiell, artist.
Delft. Painted blue. 1764. (c) HOLLAND. De Oude Moriaan's
Hooft (The Old Moor's Head). Delft. 1759. (d) HOLLAND. De
Ster (The Star). A. Kiell, artist. Delft. 1763. (e) HOLLAND. De
Witte Ster (The White Star). Delft. Painted blue. 1764. (f) HOL-
LAND. A Kiell, artist. Delft. Painted blue. 1764.

g   h   i   j   k   l

(g) HOLLAND. De Ster (The Star). A. Kiell, artist. Delft. 1764.
(h) HOLLAND. Q. Kleynoven. artist. Delft. Painted blue. 1680.
(i) HOLLAND. A. Kiell, artist. Delft. Painted blue. 1764. (j) HOL-
LAND. De Griekse A (The Greek A). A. Korks, artist. Delft. 1687.
(k) ALCORA, Spain. Porcelain. Painted red, gold, black, or incised.
From 1784. (l) AICH. Germany. Porcelain. From 1849.

m   n   o   p   q   r

(m) ALT-ROHLAU, Bohemia. A. Nowotny, artist. Pottery and hard
paste porcelain. Impressed blue. Circa 1823. (n) MOUSTIERS,
France. Fayence. 18th century. (o) MOSCOW, Russia. 1806-1872.
(p) HOLLAND. De Twee Scheepjes (The Two Ships). A. Pennus.
Delft. 1759. (q) APREY, France. Pottery. Painted black. 1750.
(r) APREY, France. Fayence. 1750.

a   b   c   d   e   f

(a) APREY, France. Pottery. Painted black. 1750. (b) HOLLAND.
De Twee Scheepjes (The Two Ships). A. Pennus. Fayence. Delft.
Circa 1760. (c) MOSCOW, Russia. A. Popoff. Hard paste. Painted.
1805-1872. (d) ANSBACH, Bavaria. J. A. Hannong. Hard paste.
Painted blue. 1718. (e) APREY, France. Fayence. Est. 1750. (f)
BOHEMIA. Hegewald. 1850.

g   h   i   j   k   l

(g) APREY, France. Fayence. Est. 1750. (h) HOLLAND. Keyser
and Pynaker. Pottery. Fayence. Delft. Painted blue. 1680. (i) HOL-
LAND. Keyser and Pynaker. Fayence. Delft. Painted color. 1680.
(j) APREY, France. Fayence. Est. 1750. (k) APREY, France. Fayence. Est. 1750. (l) ARRAS, France. Soft paste. Est. 1770.

m   n   o   p   q   r

(m) ARRAS, France. Soft paste. Est. 1770. (n) PARIS, France.
Claude Reverend. Fayence. 1664. (o) MEISSEN, Germany. Hard
paste. Painted blue underglaze. Circa 1725. (p) MEISSEN, Ger-
many. Helene Wolfsohn, decorator. Circa 1860. (q) MEISSEN,
Germany. Helene Wolfsohn, decorator. Hard paste. Painted blue.
Circa 1860. (r) PARIS, France. Pottery. Painted blue. 1664.

a   b   c   d   e

(a) MEILLONAS, France. Fayence. Est. 1745. (b) HOLLAND.
Fayence. Delft. Painted blue. 1680. (c) ANSBACH, Bavaria. J. A.
Hannong. Hard paste. Painted blue. Circa 1700. (d) EISENACH,
Germany. A. Saeltzer. Est. 1858. (e) HOLLAND. A. J. v. d. Meer.
Fayence. Delft. 1671.

f   g   h   i   j

(f) GREAT BRITAIN. Don Pottery. Pottery. 1790. (g) HOL-
LAND. A. Kiell. Delft. Painted blue. 1764. (h) HOLLAND. Fay-
ence. Delft. Painted. Circa 1700. (i) NORWICH, Connecticut,
U.S.A. Armstrong and Wentworth. Impressed. 1812-1834. (j) AICH,
Germany. Porcelain. Artist's initials. Circa 1849.

k   l   m   n

(k) HOLLAND. De Ster (The Star). J. Aalmes. Fayence. Delft.
Est. 1690. (l) BURSLEM, Great Britain. Pottery. Impressed. 1750.
(m) SOUTH AMBOY, New Jersey, U.S.A. Cadmus. Impressed.
Circa 1850. (n) STOKE-ON-TRENT, Great Britain. U.S.A. William Adams II. 1829.

ADAMS   ADAMS & Co.   Adams & Co.

a   b   c

(a) TUNSTALL, Great Britain. Printed ware, stoneware, jaspers.
1787-1810. (b) TUNSTALL, Great Britain. Jasper ware. Impressed.
Circa 1790. (c) TUNSTALL, Great Britain. Creamware. Impressed.
Circa 1790.

ADAMS   ADAMS   A.D. HIGGINS
ENGLAND   TUNSTALL   CLEVELAND
                                         OHIO

d   e   f

(d) TUNSTALL, Great Britain. Printed. 19th century. (e) TUN-
STALL, Great Britain. Impressed. 19th century. (f) CLEVELAND,
Ohio, U.S.A. A. D. Higgins. Impressed. 1837-1850.

ADMIRAL   A.J. BUTLER & Co.
———————— A.G.C. DIPPLE   Aich   NEW BRUNSWICK
V. P.CO. LEWISBURG, PA.   N. J.

g   h   i   j

(g) EAST LIVERPOOL, Ohio, U.S.A. Vodrey Brothers. 1857-1885.
(h) LEWISBURG, Pennsylvania, U.S.A. A. G. Dipple. Impressed.
Circa 1890. (i) AICH, Germany. Porcelain. Impressed. Circa 1849.
(j) NEW BRUNSWICK, New Jersey, U.S.A. A. J. Butler and Company. Impressed. Circa 1850.

a   b   c   d

(a) PARIS, France. A. Jean. Fayence. 1859. (b) EAST LIVER-
POOL, Ohio, U.S.A. East End Pottery Company. 20th century. (c)
BURSLEM, Great Britain. Staffordshire. 1830. (d) ALCORA, Spain.
Soliva, painter. Fayence. Est. 1750.

e   f   g

(e) GREENSBORO, Pennsylvania, U.S.A. Alexander Boughner.
Impressed. 1812-1850. (f) LIMOGES, France. Est. 1774. (g) EAST
LIVERPOOL, Ohio, U.S.A. William Brunt Pottery Company. 1850-
1894.

ALMA   [ALPINE CHINA]   AMBERG   AMERICAN CHINA
                                                    A C CO

h   i   j   k

(h) EVANSVILLE, Indiana, U.S.A. Crown Pottery Company. Est.
1891. (i) EAST LIVERPOOL, Ohio, U.S.A. William Brunt Pottery
Company. 1850-1894. (j) AMBERG, Germany. Late 19th century.
(k) TRENTON, New Jersey, U.S.A. American Crockery Company.
Est. 1876.

a   b   c

(**a**) JERSEY CITY, New Jersey, U.S.A. American Pottery Company. Printed. 1833-1845. (**b**) JERSEY CITY, New Jersey, U.S.A. American Pottery Company. Printed. Circa 1830. (**c**) JERSEY CITY, New Jersey, U.S.A. American Pottery Company. Impressed or printed. Circa 1830.

a moulins   Amstel   Amstel.   ᴬNCHOᴿ JEN

d   e   f   g

(**d**) MOULINS, France. Fayence. 18th century. (**e**) HOLLAND. Amstel Niewer. Hard paste. Painted blue. Circa 1800. (**f**) HOLLAND. Oude Amstel. Hard paste. Painted blue. 1782. (**g**) TRENTON, New Jersey, U.S.A. Anchor Pottery Company. Printed. Circa 1890.

ANTHONY SCOTT   ANTHONY SHAW
& SONS   BURSLEM   A PEYRAU

h   i   j

(**h**) SUNDERLAND, Great Britain. Anthony Scott and Sons. Circa 1835. (**i**) BURSLEM, Great Britain. 1850. (**j**) NEW YORK CITY, New York, U.S.A. A. Peyrau. 1891.

Apiello A.P.M. C° ARENDDEHAAK JS.

    a   b   c   d

(a) CAPO-DI-MONTE, Italy. Soft paste. Incised. Circa 1760. (b) GLOUCESTER, New Jersey. U.S.A. American Porcelain Manufacturing Company. Soft paste. Impressed. 1855. (c) EAST LIVERPOOL, Ohio, U.S.A. Vodrey Brothers. 1857-1885. (d) HOLLAND. A. D. Haak. Fayence. Delft. 1780.

ARMSTRONG + WENTWORTH
NORWICH   ASHFIELD   ASTBURY a$t_wn ne

    e   f   g   h

(e) NORWICH, Connecticut, U.S.A. Armstrong and Wentworth. Impressed. 1814-1834. (f) ASHFIELD, Massachusetts, U.S.A. Hastings and Belding. Impressed. 1850-1855. (g) SHELTON, Great Britain. Astbury Pottery. Impressed. Circa 1830. (h) HOLLAND. De Drie Astonnen (The Three Ash Barrels). G. P. Kam. Fayence. Delft. 1674.

A Sverin   Aurelain   A&W BOUGHNER
  K   WELLER   GREENSBORO
                      PA.   AVALON

    i   j   k   l

(i) SCHWERIN, Germany. Fayence. 1760. (j) ZANESVILLE, Ohio, U.S.A. S. A. Weller. Late 19th century. (k) GREENSBORO, Pennsylvania, U.S.A. A. and W. Boughner. Impressed, blue. 1850-1890. (l) EAST LIVERPOOL, Ohio, U.S.A. Cartwright Brothers. 1880-1900.

a   b   c   d

(a) HOLLAND. De Lampetkan (The Ewer). Fayence. Delft. 1780.
(b) TOURS, France. Est. 1842. (c) CINCINNATI, Ohio, U.S.A.
Avon Pottery. Est. 1886. (d) NOCKAMIXON, Pennsylvania, U.S.A.
Abraham Weaver. 1824-1844.

SECTION B
See also Sections
H, E, Lines

B   B   *B*   *B*   B   B

e   f   g   h   i   j

(e) WORCESTER, Great Britain, Barr. Porcelain. 1793-1803. (f)
MARSEILLES, France. Pottery. Painted. 1769. (g) WORCESTER,
Great Britain. Barr. 1793-1803. (h) POLAND. Belvedere. 1774-1800.
(i) TRENTON, New Jersey, U.S.A. Isaac Broome. Est. 1880. (j)
WORCESTER, Great Britain. Barr. Porcelain. 1793-1803.

k   l   m   n   o   p

(k) KIEL, Germany. Fayence. Circa 1770. (l) BOISSETTE,
France. Circa 1777. (m) WORCESTER, Great Britain. Flight and
Barr. Incised. 1792-1807. (n) BOW, Great Britain. Porcelain. 1744-
1776. (o) LILLE, France. Fayence. 1720-1778. (p) HOLLAND.
De Porceleyne Byl (The Porcelain Hatchet). J. Brouwer. Fayence.
Delft. 1759.

a   b   c   d   e   f

(a) FRANKENTHAL, Germany. Est. 1755. (b) BRISTOL, Great
Britain. Hard paste. Painted. 1773. (c) HOLLAND. J. Brouwer.
Pottery. Painted blue. 1750. (d) BOISSETTE, France. Underglaze
blue. Circa 1778. (e) BUDAU, Germany. 1825. (f) BOISSETTE,
France. 1777.

g   h   i   j   k

(g-h) BRISTOL, Great Britain. Pottery or porcelain. Blue or gold.
18th century. (i) BRISTOL, Great Britain. Porcelain. 1765-1782.
(j) BRISTOL, Great Britain. Pottery or porcelain. Blue or gold.
18th century. (k) BRISTOL, Great Britain. Hard paste. Blue or
gold. 1773.

l   m   n   o   p

(l) PINXTON, Great Britain. Soft paste. 1796. (m) TOURNAY,
France. Est. 18th century. (n-o) BRISTOL, Great Britain. Porcelain.
1773. (p) NIDERVILLER, France. Hard paste. Circa 1758.

a   b   c   d

(a) BRUSSELS, Belgium. 1780. (b) NIDERVILLER, France.
Circa 1758. (c) MOUSTIERS, France. Fayence. 1778. (d) HO-
HENSTEIN, Germany. Porcelain. Circa 1850.

e   f   g   h   i

(e) ST. CLOUD, France. J. B. Chicaneau, founder. Porcelain.
Painted. Circa 1700. (f) NIDERVILLER, France. Hard Paste. Est.
1758. (g) ROUEN, France. Duprey. Fayence. 1800. (h) ROUEN,
France. Duprey. 1800. (i) ST. AMAND-LES-EAUX, France. Fayence. Est. 1718.

j   k   l   m

(j) LILLE, France. Francois Boussemart. Fayence. 1729-1773.
(k) BAYREUTH, Germany. Frankel and Schreck. Circa 1745.
(l) COPENHAGEN, Denmark. Bing and Grondahl. 1853. (m)
BAYREUTH, Germany. Knöller. Fayence. Circa 1730.

a   b   c   d   e

(**a**) ROUEN, France. Duprey. Fayence. 1800. (**b**) BAYREUTH,
Germany. Porcelain. Circa 1800. (**c-d**) BAYREUTH, Germany.
Knoller. Fayence. Circa 1745. (**e**) LUXEMBOURG. Belgium. Por-
celain. Painted. 1806.

f   g   h   i   j   k

(**f**) LIMBACH, Germany. Porcelain. Est. 1773. (**g-h**) LUXEM-
BOURG, Belgium. Boch, director. Pottery and hard paste. Painted.
1806. (**i-j**) ALENCELON, France. Brancas. Hard paste. Circa 1763.
(**k**) LIMBACH, Germany. Porcelain. Est. 1773.

l   m   n   o   p

(**l**) ORLEANS, France. Gold or blue. Benoist le Brun. 1808-1811.
(**m-n-o**) LIMBACH, Germany. Porcelain. Est. 1773. (**p**) MOUS-
TIERS, France. Joseph Olery. Fayence. 1738.

| a | b | c | d | e |

(**a**) ORLEANS, France. Benoist Le Brun. 1808-1811. (**b-c**) TREN-
TON, New Jersey, U.S.A. Burroughs and Mountford. 1879-1882.
(**d**) HOLLAND. De Vergulde Bloompot (The Golden Flowerpot).
Fayence. Delft. 1759. (**e**) HOLLAND. De Vergulde Bloompot (The
Golden Flowerpot). Fayence. Delft. 1761.

| f | g | h | i | j |

(**f-g**) BAYREUTH, Germany. Pfeiffer. Fayence. 1760-1767. (**h**)
ALCORA, Spain. Porcelain. Est. 1727. (**i**) MARANS, France. Jean
Pierre Roussencq. Pottery. Est. 1740. (**j**) BOURG-LA-REINE,
France. Est. 1773.

BЯ   B.R.   BR   BS.&T.

| k | l | m | n |

(**k-l-m**) BOURG-LA-REINE, France. Soft paste. Est. 1773. (**n**)
BURSLEM, Great Britain. Barker, Sutton, and Till. 1830-1850.

B. V.

a   b   c   d   e

(a) PARIS, France. M. Victor Barbizet. Fayence, 1850. (b-c) NI-
DERVILLER, France. Baron de Beyerle, founder. Hard Paste.
Painted. 1754. (d) LIMBACH, Germany. Porcelain. Est. 1772 (e)
HOLLAND. De Klauw (The Claw). Fayence. Delft. 1702.

f   g   h   i

(f) ZURICH, Switzerland. Porcelain and fayence. Est. 1763. (g)
TUNSTALL, Great Britain. Benjamin Adams. 1805-1820 (h) SHEL-
TON, Great Britain. Pottery. Impressed. Circa 1760. (i) LONG-
TON, Great Britain. Bailey and Batkin. Est. 1751.

BARKER

j   k   l   m

(j) SWANSEA, Great Britain. Baker, Bevans and Irwin. 1813-1839.
(k) TRENTON, New Jersey, U.S.A. Burgess and Campbell. Est.
1870. (l) FENTON, Great Britain. Pottery. Circa 1790. (m)
CHARLESTOWN, Massachusetts, U.S.A. Edmunds and Company.
Impressed. Circa 1856.

FRANCE LIMOGES

Barr Flight & Barr

👑 🍀
BARR FLIGHT & BARR.
Royal Porcelain Works.
WORCESTER.
London House.
N°.1 Coventry Street.

a   b   c

(a) LIMOGES, France. Circa 1870. (b-c) WORCESTER, Great Britain. Hard paste. Printed. 1807-1813.

BARR FLIGHT & BARR
Royal Porcelain Works
WORCESTER
London House
No 1 Coventry Street

BARTOL ᴬᴹᴱᴼ**Botero**

BATHWELL GOODFELLOW

d   e   f

(d) WORCESTER, Great Britain. Hard paste. Printed. 1807-1813. (e) SAVONO, Italy. 1728. (f) BURSLEM, Great Britain. Impressed. Circa 1810.

Bäyreith 1744

Bayr: K. C.

B B NEWSTONE

B-C WILTON

g   h   i   j

(g) BAYREUTH, Germany. J. F. Metzsch, decorator. 1744. (h) BAYREUTH, Germany. Knoller. Fayence. 1728-1744. (i) STOKE-ON-TRENT, Great Britain. Minton. Hard paste. 1845-1861. (j) TRENTON, New Jersey, U.S.A. International Pottery Company. Est. 1870.

BELL CHINA   BELPER POTTERY
B P C?

BELL   Findlay, Ohio   DENBY

a   b   c

(a) STRASBURG, Virginia, U.S.A. Samuel and Solomon Bell. 1852-1883. (b) FINDLAY, Ohio, U.S.A. Bell Pottery Company. 19th century. (c) DERBYSHIRE, Great Britain. Belper Pottery. Stoneware. 1812.

BENNETT & CHOLLAR
HOMER

Berlin
ANCHOR POTTERY

BERLIN
C A & SONS
ENGLAND.

d   e   f   g

(d) HULL, Great Britain. Bellevue Pottery Company. 1825. (e) HOMER, New York, U.S.A. Bennett and Chollar. Impressed. 1843. (f) TRENTON, New Jersey, U.S.A. Anchor Pottery Company. Circa 1895. (g) HULL, Great Britain. Bellevue Pottery Company. Est. 1802.

BEVINGTON & CO.
SWANSEA

Beyerock

Biloxi

h   i   j   k

(h) TRENTON, New Jersey, U.S.A. Glasgow Pottery Company. Circa 1870. (i) SWANSEA, Wales. Porcelain. 1814-1822. (j) BEYERECK, Germany. Stoneware. Circa 1824. (k) EAST BILOXI, Mississippi, U.S.A. George Ohr. 1890-1900.

Birch   B. J. KRUMEICH
             NEWARK
             N.J.   BLAIR
                            CORTLAND, N.Y.   BlaR

a   b   c   d

(**a**) HANLEY, Great Britain. E. J. Birch. Staffordshire. Circa 1800.
(**b**) NEWARK, New Jersey, U.S.A. B. J. Krumeich. Circa 1850.
(**c**) CORTLAND, New York, U.S.A. Sylvester Blair. 1828-1836.
(**d**) BOURG-LA-REINE, France. Soft paste and pottery. Painted
blue. 1773.

BLONDEL   6 Compot   Bochet Buschmann
                            a Mettlach   Booth

e   f   g   h

(**e**) DOUAI, France. Est. 1781. (**f**) HOLLAND. De Vergulde
Bloompot (The Golden Flowerpot). Fayence. Delft. Circa 1693.
(**g**) METTLACH, Germany. Fayence. 19th century. (**h**) TUN-
STALL, Great Britain. Enoch Booth. Pottery. Impressed. 1750.

BOOTH & SONS   Bordeaux
                 Mercer   Borgano   Borne
                                           Pinxit
                                           Anno
                                           1738

i   j   k   l

(**i**) STOKE-ON-TRENT, Great Britain. Booth and Sons. 1803. (**j**)
TRENTON, New Jersey, U.S.A. Mercer Pottery Company. Circa
1870. (**k**) TURIN, Italy. Fayence. 18th century. (**l**) ROUEN,
France. Claude Borne. Fayence. 1738.

BOSS BROS.
MIDDLEBURY
OHIO

BOOTHWELL
GOODFELLOW

BOTT & CO

a   b   c

(a) AKRON, Ohio, U.S.A. Boss Brothers. Impressed. Circa 1875.
(b) TUNSTALL, Great Britain. 1828. (c) GREAT BRITAIN. Bott
and Company. Staffordshire. Early 19th century.

J. Boulard a Nevers
1622

BOURNE'S
POTTERIES

BOURNE'S POTTERIES
DENBY & CODNOR PARK
DERBYSHIRE

d   e   f

(d) NEVERS, France. J. Boulard, potter. 1622. (e) DERBYSHIRE,
Great Britain. Stoneware. Circa 1800. (f) DERBYSHIRE, Great
Britain. Stoneware. 19th century.

BOURNE, NIXON & CO

BOUTET

B. Plant

B
Potter
42

g   h   i   j

(g) TUNSTALL, Great Britain. Bourne, Nixon, and Company.
Circa 1830. (h) AUXERRE, France. (Yonne.) Est. 1799. (i) LANE
END, Great Britain. Pottery. Impressed. 1777. (j) PARIS, France.
Christopher Potter. Circa 1790.

a   b   c   d

(a) PRAGUE, Bohemia. Prager. Lead-glazed earthenware. 1810-
1862. (b) SWINTON, Great Britain. (Rockingham factory.) John
and William Brameld, potters. Late 18th and 19th centuries. (c)
BURTON-ON-TRENT, Great Britain. Tooth and Company. 20th
century. (d) LIMBACH, Germany. Porcelain. Est. 1722.

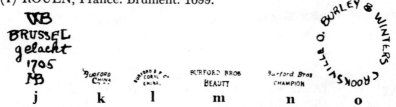

e   f   g   h   i

(e) BRISTOL, Great Britain. Porcelain. Circa 1750. (f) EAST
LIVERPOOL, Ohio, U.S.A. Cartwright Brothers. Circa 1900. (g)
TRENTON, New Jersey, U.S.A. Isaac Broome. Est. 1880. (h) EAST
HAMPTON, New York, U.S.A. Middle Lane Pottery. Circa 1900.
(i) ROUEN, France. Brument. 1699.

j   k   l   m   n   o

(j) BRUSSELS, Belgium. Fayence. 1705. (k-l-m-n) EAST LIVER-
POOL, Ohio, U.S.A. Burford Brothers Pottery Company. 1880 (o)
CROOKSVILLE, Ohio, U.S.A. Burley and Winters. Circa 1850.

a   b   c   d   e   f

(a) CHODAU, Germany. Est. 1805. (b) NANTES, France. Est. 1780. (c-d-e-f) CAUGHLEY, Great Britain. Est. 1750.

g   h   i   j   k   l

(g-h-i) CAUGHLEY, Great Britain. Est. 1750. (j) DOCCIA, Italy. Est. 1737. (k) BAYREUTH, Germany. Hard Paste. Painted. 1744. (l) BAYREUTH, Germany. Hard Paste. Painted. 1744.

m   n   o   p   q

(m) CASTEL-DURANTE, Italy. Est. 1570. (n) HOLLAND. De Ster (The Star). C. D. Berg. Fayence. Delft. 1720. (o) COAL-BROOKDALE, Great Britain. Hard Paste. Painted blue. Circa 1825-1850. (p) HOLLAND. De Ster (The Star). C. D. Berg. Fayence. Delft. 1720. (q) HOLLAND. De Jonge Moriaan's Hooft (The New Moor's Head). H. Strale. 1764.

Gc $\overline{\underset{\text{C.P.}}{ccc}}$ C·D L·D C:Ɔ

a   b   c   d   e

(a) ST. PETERSBURG, Russia. Hard Paste. Painted blue. 1765.
(b) TERVUEREN, Belguim. Fayence. 1720. (c-d) LIMOGES,
France. Hard Paste. Painted red. 1773. (e) LIMOGES, France.
Hard paste. 1773.

6.D.   ℘   C&F   **C.F.** $\overset{\text{XI}}{\underset{4}{CF}}$ C G

f   g   h   i   j   k

(f-g) COALBROOKDALE, Great Britain. Hard paste. Painted
blue. 1787. (h) SCOTLAND. Circa 1850. (i-j) PIRKENHAMMER,
Germany. Christian Fischer. Hard paste. 1846-1853. (k) LEEDS,
Great Britain. Est. 1760.

C&G $\overset{CG}{W}$ CH   C·H   CH   C.H

l   m   n   o   p   q

(l) STOKE-ON-TRENT, Great Britain. Copeland and Garrett.
1833-1847. (m) LEEDS, Great Britain. Est. 1760. (n) STRAS-
BOURG, France. Fayence. Incised. 1721-1739. (o) PARIS, France.
Hard paste. Painted red. 1784. (p) ROCKHILL, Pennsylvania,
U.S.A. Charles Headman. 1840-1870. (q) PARIS, France. Chanou.
1746-1779.

a b c d e f

(a) NEW YORK, New York, U.S.A. Carr and Morrison. 1855. (b) BUCKSVILLE, Pennsylvania, U.S.A. Christian Klinker. Circa 1780. (c) MORRISVILLE, Pennsylvania, U.S.A. Robertson Art Tile Company. 19th century. (d) CHELSEA, Massachusetts, U.S.A. Chelsea Keramic Art Works. Impressed. 1875-1889. (e) HOLLAND. De Metale Pot (The Metal Pot). L. Cleffius. Fayence. Delft. 1667. (f) PARIS, France. Marie-Anne Chicaneau. 1741.

g h i j k l

(g) ST. CLOUD, France. Fayence. Porcelain. Circa 1711. (h) FLORSHEIM, Germany. Fayence. Circa 1780. (i) NYON, Switzerland. Hard paste. Painted blue. 1780. (j) NEW ORLEANS, Louisiana, U.S.A. Newcomb Pottery. Circa 1895. (k) NIDERVILLE, France. Custine. Hard paste. 1770-1793. (l) TELECHANY, Poland. Count Michael Oginski. Late 18th century.

m n o p q r

(m) CREPY-EN-VALOIS, France. 1762. (n) SINCENY, France. Pottery. Painted color. 1733. (o) MARSEILLES, France. Savy. Fayence. 1770. (p-q) THURINGIA. Germany. Kloster Veilsdorf. Porcelain. Est. 1760. (r) GREENPOINT, New York, U.S.A. Volkmar Keramic Company. Circa 1880.

C. V. ♂

ⒸⓍﾉ   C : V : S   ‾‾192‾‾   caen   CAEN

a   b   c   d   e

(a-b) HOLLAND. De Oude Moriaan's Hooft (The Old Moor's
Head). G. Verstelle. Fayence. Delft. 1764. (c) HOLLAND. De
Klauw (The Claw). C. V. Schoonhove. Fayence. Delft. 1668. (d)
CAEN, France. Hard paste. Painted red. 1793. (e) CAEN, France.
Hard paste. 1793.

AHRENFELDT   CALLAND
C. LIMOGES   CALEB CRAFTS   SWANSEA   CAMBRIAN

f   g   h   i

(f) LIMOGES, France. 1842-1898. (g) PORTLAND, Maine, U.S.A.
Caleb Crafts. Impressed. Circa 1840. (h) SWANSEA, Great Britain.
John F. Calland. Circa 1845. (i) SWANSEA, Great Britain. Hard
paste. Painted color. 1765.

                      CANTON
CAMP & THOMPSON   CHINA   c. aprey

j   k   l

(j) AKRON. Ohio, U.S.A. Camp and Thompson. Impressed. 1870-
1880. (k). STEUBENVILLE, Ohio, U.S.A. Steubenville Pottery
Company. Est. 1879. (l) APREY, France. Fayence, Est. 1744.

Carl ✳ Gr   **CARL KNOLL**
              CARLSBAD ⁵⁺ᶠ   Carlo Coccore se

a   b   c

(a) BUEN RETIRO, Spain. Soft paste. 1759-1808. (b) FISCHERN, Bohemia. 1848. (c) NAPLES, Italy. Circa 1785.

CARLSBAD   **CAULDON**   CAULDON England

d   e   f

(d) FISCHERN, Bohemia. Porcelain. 1848. (e) SHELTON, Great Britain. Ridgways. Circa 1850. (f) SHELTON, Great Britain. Circa 1900.

C. CROLIUS
MANUFACTURER
NEW YORK   CDale   C DILLON & Co   CFH
                         ALBANY   GDM

g   h   i   j

(g) NEW YORK. New York, U.S.A. Clarkson Crolius, Senior. Circa 1840. (h) COALBROOKDALE, Great Britain. Circa 1830. (i) ALBANY, New York, U.S.A. C. Dillon and Company. Circa 1830. (j) FRANCE. E. Gerard Dufraissein et Morel. 1882-1898.

a   b   c   d

(a) FRANCE. E. Gerard Dufraissein et Morel. Whiteware. 1882-1898. (b) MEISSEN, Germany. 1750. (c) HANOVER, Pennsylvania. Greber Pottery. Circa 1850. (d) WORCESTER, Great Britain. Impressed, printed. 1847-1850.

e   f   g

(e) WORCESTER, Great Britain. 1788-1808. (f) WORCESTER. Great Britain. 1847. (g) WORCESTER, Great Britain. 1814-1820.

h   i   j

(h) WORCESTER, Great Britain. 1814. (i) WORCESTER, Great Britain. 1840-1845. (j) WORCESTER, Great Britain. 1820-1840.

Champion

CHAS ALLERTON & SONS
ENGLAND

Chas. Headman

a　　　　　　　　　b　　　　　　　　　c

(a) EAST LIVERPOOL, Ohio, U.S.A. United States Pottery. Est.
1846. (b) LONGTON, Great Britain, Charles Allerton. Circa 1900.
(c) ROCKHILL, Pennsylvania, U.S.A. Charles Headman. Circa
1825.

Chatillon　　　*Chelsea*
　　　　　　　　　1745

CHELSEA KERAMIC
ART WORKS
ROBERTSON & SONS

d　　　　　　　　e　　　　　　　　f

(d)CHATILLON, France. Hard paste. Est. 1775. (e) CHELSEA,
Great Britain. Soft paste. 1745. (f) CHELSEA, Massachusetts,
U.S.A. Chelsea Keramic Art Works. 1866.

Chester　　CHETHAM　　*Chetham & Woolley*
　　　　　　　　　　　　　Lane End 1798

CHICAGO

g　　　　h　　　　　　i　　　　　　j

(g) EAST LIVERPOOL, Ohio, U.S.A. William Brunt Pottery Company. Circa 1875. (h) LANE END, Great Britain. Staffordshire.
1795. (i) LANE END, Great Britain. Staffordshire. 1798. (j) EAST
LIVERPOOL, Ohio, U.S.A. William Brunt Pottery Company. Circa
1875.

CHILD   Chodau   CHOLLAR & DARBY
                                                         HOMER, N.Y.

a   b   c   d

(a) TUNSTALL, Great Britain. Smith Child, potter. Cream-colored
ware. Impressed. Late 18th century. (b) PARIS, France. Porcelain.
1795. (c) CHODAU, Germany. Est. 1805. (d) HOMER, New York,
U.S.A. Chollar and Darby. Impressed. Circa 1845.

C A. PILLIVUT   CHRISTIAN LINK
&C^ PARIS   Christian   STONETOWN   CLEM HAMILTON

e   f   g   h

(e) FOECY, France. Pillivuyt family, potters. 19th and 20th centuries. (f) LIVERPOOL, Great Britain. Pottery. Impressed. 1765.
(g) STONETOWN, Pennsylvania, U.S.A. Christian Link. Impressed. Circa 1870. (h) TUSCARAWAS COUNTY, Ohio, U.S.A.
Clem Hamilton. Impressed. Circa 1870.

CLOSE & C°
Late
              C.LINK   W. ADAMS 8 SONS
C.LINK   EXETER   STOKE-UPON-TRENT   Coalport.

i   j   k   l

(i-j) STONETOWN, Pennsylvania. U.S.A. Christian Link. Impressed. Circa 1870. (k) STOKE-ON-TRENT, Great Britain. Impressed. Circa 1829. (l) COALBROOKDALE, Great Britain. Hard
paste. Painted blue. Circa 1825.

COCHRAN & FLEMING   COLUMBIAN   COMMRAW   COMMERAW: 8
GLASGOW   TRENTON   STONEWARE
                     N. J.   NEW YORK
                     ART POTTERY

a   b   c   d

(a) GLASGOW, Scotland. Cochran and Fleming. Circa 1860. (b)
TRENTON, New Jersey, U.S.A. Columbian Art Pottery. Est. 1875.
(c-d) CORLEAR'S HOOK, New York, U.S.A. Thomas Commeraw.
Circa 1810.

Copeland   COPELAND & GARRETT   COPELAND   Copeland
                                    B   Late Spode.

e   f   g   h

(e) STOKE-ON-TRENT, Great Britain. Hard paste and pottery.
Impressed. 1847. (f) STOKE-ON-TRENT, Great Britain. 1833-
1847. (g) STOKE-ON-TRENT, Great Britain. 1847. (h) STOKE-
ON-TRENT, Great Britain. W. T. Copeland and Sons. 1847-1867.

CORLEAR'S HOOK   CORTLAND   C. P. CO.   C. P. Co.
                                          CHINA

i   j   k   l

(i) CORLEAR'S HOOK, New York, U.S.A. Impressed. Circa 1800.
(j) CORTLAND, New York, U.S.A. Sylvester Blair. Circa 1830.
(k) GREENOCK, Scotland. Clyde Pottery Company. 1900. (l)
CHITTENANGO, New York, U.S.A. Chittenango Pottery Company.
Circa 1900.

C.P.Co. CHITTENANGO.N.Y. CHINA	C.P Co LTD	C. P. CO. REX	C. P. CO. ROYAL	CREMORNE OPAQUE PORCELAIN
a	b	c	d	e

(a) CHITTENANGO, New York, U.S.A. Chittenango Pottery Company. Circa 1900. (b) PHOENIXVILLE, Pennsylvania, U.S.A. Chester Pottery Company. Est. 1894. (c-d) EVANSVILLE, Indiana, U.S.A. Crown Pottery Company. Circa 1895. (e) BALTIMORE, Maryland, U.S.A. Maryland Pottery Company. Circa 1880.

crepy	Crown Porcelain.	C.Crette.de Bruxelle. aue D'Aremberg 791	C.TUPPER PORTAGE CO. O.
f	g	h	i

(f) CREPY-EN-VALOIS, France. Incised. 1764. (g) EVANSVILLE, Indiana, U.S.A. Crown Pottery Company. Circa 1895. (h) BRUSSELS, Belguim. Louis Cretté. Hard paste. Painted color. 1791-1803. (i) PORTAGE COUNTY, Ohio, U.S.A. C. Tupper. Impressed. Circa 1870.

CYFFLÉ A LUNÉVILLE.	Cyples	CYPLES & BARKER
j	k	l

(j) LUNEVILLE, France. Fayence. 1758. (k) LONGTON, Great Britain. Cyples, potter. Late 18th and early 19th centuries. (l) LONGTON, Great Britain. Staffordshire. Circa 1800.

Section **D**
See also Sections
O, Lines

a   b   c   d   e   f

(a) DAVENPORT, Great Britain. Impressed. 1793-1882. (b) DERBY, Great Britain. 1770-1784. (c) CAUGHLEY, Great Britain. Hard paste. Painted blue. Est. 1750. (d) DALLWITZ, Bohemia. W. W. Lorenz. Circa 1832. (e) HOLLAND. De Griekse A (The Greek A). J. T. Dextra. Fayence. Delft. 1759. (f) NORD, France. Valenciennes. Louis Dorez. Fayence. 1735.

g   h   i   j   k

(g) NORD, France. Valenciennes. Louis Dorez. 1735. (h) DERBY, Great Britain. Soft paste. Painted red. 1756. (i) DRYVILLE, Pennsylvania, U.S.A. John Dry (Drey). Circa 1825. (j) WORCESTER, Great Britain. John Donaldson, painter. Porcelain. 1737-1810. (k) DERBY, Great Britain. 1782.

l   m   n   o   p

(l) DERBY, Great Britain. 1770. (m) LILLE, France. Pottery. Painted color. Circa 1745. (n) HOLLAND. De Griekse A (The Greek A). J. T. Dextra. Fayence. Delft. 1759. (o) HOLLAND. De Paauw (The Peacock). D. Kam. Fayence. Delft. 1697. (p) HOLLAND. De Paauw (The Peacock). Jacobus de Milde. Fayence. Delft. 1651.

a   b   c   d   e

(a) HOLLAND. Fayence. Delft. 1764. (b) HOLLAND. De Paauw
(The Peacock). Jacobus de Milde. Registered 1764. (c) MEN-
NECY-VILLEROY, France. Soft paste. 1734. (d) TRENTON, New
Jersey, U.S.A. Prospect Hill Pottery Company. Circa 1880. (e)
NEVERS, France. Denis Lefebvre. Pottery. Painted. 17th century.

Dk DL D $\underset{1636}{\overline{\text{ILF}}}$ $DP.$

f   g   h   i   j

(f) HOLLAND. De Paauw (The Peacock). D. Kam. Fayence.
Delft. 1697. (g) LONGTON HALL, Great Britain. William Littler,
potter. Staffordshire. 1750-1760. (h) NORD, France. Valenciennes.
Louis Dorez. 1735. (i) NEVERS, France. Denis Lefebvre. 1636.
(j) SILESIA, Germany. Proskau. Fayence. Dietrichstein period.
1770-1783.

$D\mathcal{P}W$ DSK $\underset{4}{\overline{DSK}}$ $.D.V.$ $\overset{\square V \, \theta}{3}$

k   l   m   n   o

(k) HOLLAND. De Paauw (The Peacock). Fayence. Delft. 1701.
(l-m) HOLLAND. De Dubbelde Schenkkan (The Double Jug).
Fayence. Delft. 1764. (n) MENNECY-VILLEROY, France. Soft
paste. Painted and incised. Est. 1734. (o) HOLLAND. De Roos
(The Rose). Fayence. Delft. 1759.

a   b   c   d   e

(**a**) HOLLAND, De Fortuyn (The Fortune). P. V. D. Briel. Fayence. Delft. 1759. (**b**) HOLLAND. D. van der Does. Fayence. Delft. Registered 1764. (**c-d**) PARIS, France. Dagoty, potter. Hard paste. Painted red. 1822. (**e**) TRENTON, New Jersey, U.S.A. Crescent Pottery Company. Est. 1881.

DALTON POTTERY   DALWITZ   DARTE FRERES A' PARIS

f   g   h

(**f**) DALTON, Ohio, U.S.A. Dalton Pottery Company. Impressed. 1875. (**g**) DALLWITZ, Germany. Circa 1804. (**h**) PARIS, France. Darte brothers, porcelain-makers. Stenciled red. 1795-1840.

DAVENPORT LONGPORT   David Spinner   DAWSON

i   j   k

(**i**) LONGPORT, Great Britain. Pottery. Impressed. 1793. (**j**) MELFORD, Pennsylvania, U.S.A. Circa 1810. (**k**) SUNDERLAND, Great Britain. Ford Pottery. Est. 1800.

D&C°   D. D. & Co.   O. Dry

FRANCE.   CASTLEFORD   D. DUNDERDALE & Co.

a   b   c   d

(a) LIMOGES, France. Circa 1875. (b) CASTLEFORD, Great
Britain. Pottery. Impressed. 1790. (c) CASTLEFORD, Great Brit-
ain. Pottery. Circa 1800. (d) DRYVILLE, Pennsylvania, U.S.A. Dry
Brothers. Circa 1850.

DECORATED BY

De Bloompot   Haviland&Co   Derby   D. GOODALE
                 Limoges.   DEX   HARTFORD

e   f   g   h   i

(e) HOLLAND. De Vergulde Bloompot (The Golden Flowerpot).
P. Verberg. Pottery. 1764. (f) HAVILAND, France. Decorated
ware. Red. 1915. (g) DERBY, Great Britain. 1750. (h) HOLLAND.
De Griekse A (The Greek A). T. Dextra. Fayence. Delft. 1764.
(i) HARTFORD, Connecticut, U.S.A. Daniel Goodale. Impressed.
Circa 1825.

DICKENS WARE WELLER.   Dihl   DILLWYN & CO.   Dixon & Co.

j   k   l   m

(j) ZANESVILLE, Ohio, U.S.A. S. A. Weller. Circa 1890. (k)
PARIS, France. Hard paste. Painted red. 1780. (l) SWANSEA,
Wales. Circa 1840. (m) SUNDERLAND, Great Britain. Sunder-
land Pottery. Printed. 1805.

D. METHVEN & SONS   *D. MORGAN*   *N. YORK*   **DON POTTERY**

a   b   c

(a) SCOTLAND. D. Methven and Sons. Circa 1875. (b) NEW
YORK, New York, U.S.A. D. Morgan. Impressed. Circa 1880.
(c) DON, Great Britain. Don Pottery. Pottery. Est. 1790.

DOULTON   **DOULTON**   ORESDEN   **DRESDEN**
LAMBETH   **& SLATERS**   WHITE·GRANI   **HOTEL CHINA.**
ENGLAND.   **PATENT**

d   e   f   g

(d) LAMBETH, Great Britain. Doulton. Circa 1891. (e) LAM-
BETH, Great Britain. Doulton. Est. 1872. (f-g) EAST LIVER-
POOL, Ohio, U.S.A. Potters Cooperative Company. Est. 1876.

Dʳ Frac
Antʰgruef.
Neap
1710   **DUCROZ & MILLIDGE**   **DUDSON BROTHERS**
                                   HANLEY, ENGLAND   *Duyn*

h   i   j   k

(h) NAPLES, Italy. Francesco Antonio Grue. 1731-1806. (i) LANE
END, Great Britain. Ducroz and Millidge. Circa 1850. (j) HAN-
SON, Great Britain. Dudson Brothers. Circa 1891. (k) HOL-
LAND. De Porceleyne Schootel (The Porcelain Dish). J. van Duyn.
Fayence. Delft. Painted blue. 1764.

SECTION **E**
See also Sections
B, Lines

$\mathcal{E}$ $\mathcal{E}$ **EB**   E B S $\mathcal{Ef}$ E. I. B.
1779

a   b   c   d   e   f

(a) ST. PETERSBURG, Russia, 1762-1796. (b) DERBY, Great
Britain. 1779. (c) PARIS, France. Circa 1800. (d) HOLLAND. De
Jonge Moriaan's Hooft (The New Moor's Head). Fayence. Delft.
1764. (e) MOUSTIERS, France. Fayence. 18th century. (f) HAN-
LEY, Great Britain. Impressed. 18th century.

E

E·L **M+B**

1754   **J760**   **E꜔**   EAGLE POTTERY   EAST LAKE POTTERY
                   GREENSBORO, PA   BRIDGETON, N.J.

g   h   i   j   k

(g) BOW, Great Britain. 1754. (h) BRISTOL, Great Britain. Pottery. 1760. (i) HOLLAND. Johannes Mesch. Fayence. Delft. 1680.
(j) GREENSBORO, Pennsylvania, U.S.A. James Hamilton. Stoneware. 1844-1890. (k) BRIDGETON, New Jersey, U.S.A. George
Hamlyn. Impressed. Circa 1835.

EASTWOOD   { ᴱᴮᴱᴺᴺᴱᵀᵀ *1876* ᴾᴼᵀᵀᴱᴿᵞ Cᴼ }   **E·Borne**
                                  1689   E. CHALLINOR

l   m   n   o

(l) HANLEY, Great Britain. W. Baddeley, Pottery. Impressed.
1795. (m) BALTIMORE, Maryland, U.S.A. Edwin Bennett. Circa
1870. (n) NEVERS, France. 1689. (o) BURSLEM, Great Britain.
1819.

EDGE & GROCOTT   EDWARD NORTON CO.   EDWARDS
                      BENNINGTON   D. H.
                      V. T

a   b   c

(a) GREAT BRITAIN. Edge and Grocott. Impressed. Circa 1825.
(b) BENNINGTON, Vermont, U.S.A. Edward Norton and Company. Impressed. Circa 1890. (c) FENTON, Great Britain. James
Edwards. Circa 1850.

E.&G. NASH   E. HALL   E.H. MERRILL
UTICA   NEWTON TOWNSHIP   SPRINGFIELD
              TUSCARAWAS CO.·   O.   ELECTRIC
                   O.

d   e   f   g

(d) UTICA, New York, U.S.A. E. and G. Nash. Impressed. Circa
1820. (e) NEWTON, Tuscarawas, Ohio, U.S.A. W. P. Harris. Impressed. Circa 1840. (f) SPRINGFIELD, Ohio, U.S.A. Edwin H.
Merrill. Impressed. Circa 1835. (g) EAST LIVERPOOL, Ohio,
U.S.A. Burford Brothers Pottery Company. Circa 1890.

E. & L.P. NORTON
BENNINGTON, VT.   Elsmere   Elton   E Lycett

h   i   j   k

(h) BENNINGTON, Vermont, U.S.A. E. and L. P. Norton. Impressed. Circa 1875. (i) EAST LIVERPOOL, Ohio, U.S.A. Cartwright Brothers. Circa 1890. (j) CLEVEDON, Great Britain. Sun-
flower Pottery Company. 20th century. (k) ATLANTA, Georgia,
U.S.A. Edward Lycett Circa 1900.

E. Mayer

E. MAYER & SON   ENGLAND

a   b   c

(a) HANLEY, Great Britain. Stoneware. Before 1820. (b) HAN-
LEY, Great Britain. E. Mayer and Son. 1820. (c) Word added to
all wares imported into the U.S.A. from England after 1891.

ENOCH BOOTH
1757

Enoch Wood

E. NORTON
BENNINGTON
VT.

d   e   f

(d) TUNSTALL, Great Britain. Enoch Booth. 1757. (e) BURS-
LEM, Great Britain. 1783-1790. (f) BENNINGTON, Vermont,
U.S.A. Edward Norton. Impressed. Circa 1882.

E. NORTON & CO.
BENNINGTON, VT.

ENTERPRISE
POTTERY
CO.

Crosian
WELLER

ESTE + 1783 +

g   h   i   j

(g) BENNINGTON, Vermont, U.S.A. Edward Norton and Com-
pany. Impressed. Circa 1890. (h) TRENTON, New Jersey, U.S.A.
Enterprise Pottery Company. Circa 1900. (i) ZANESVILLE, Ohio,
U.S.A. S. A. Weller. Circa 1890. (j) ESTE, Italy. Porcelain. 1783.

ESTE
G.

Etiolles
1768
Pelleve

ETRUSCAN

a　　　　　　　b　　　　　　　c

(a) ESTE, Italy. Franchini. Impressed. After 1782. (b) ETOILLES, France. Porcelain. 1770. (c) PHOENIXVILLE, Pennsylvania, U.S.A. Griffen, Smith, and Hill. Impressed. Circa 1879.

ETRUSCAN MAJOLICA

EVAN B. JONES
PITTSTON
PENNA

EVANS & GLASSON
SWANSEA
BEST GOODS
CUBA

d　　　　　　　e　　　　　　　f

(d) PHOENIXVILLE, Pennsylvania, U.S.A. Griffin, Smith, and Hill. Impressed. Est. 1879. (e) PITTSTON, Pennsylvania, U.S.A. Evan B. Jones. Impressed. Circa 1880. (f) SWANSEA, Great Britain. Evans and Glasson. Circa 1855.

E & W BENNETT
CANTON AVE.
BALTIMORE, MARYLAND

E. WENTWORTH
NORWICH

E. Wood

g　　　　　　　h　　　　　　　i

(g) BALTIMORE, Maryland, U.S.A. E. and W. Bennett. Impressed. Circa 1850. (h) NORWICH, Connecticut, U.S.A. Armstrong and Wentworth. Impressed. Circa 1820. (i) BURSLEM, Great Britain. Enoch Wood. 1783-1840.

SECTION **F**
See also Sections
P, Lines

a   b   c   d   e   f

(**a**) ROUEN, France. Fayence. 1644. (**b**) PARIS, France. Feuillet, decorator. Hard paste. 1820-1850. (**c**) FURSTENBERG, Germany. Est. 1747. (**d**) FURSTENBERG, Germany. Porcelain. Est. 1747. (**e**) FURSTENBERG. Germany. Hard paste. Painted blue. Est. 1747. (**f**) COPENHAGEN, Denmark. Jacob Fortling. Fayence. 1755-1762.

g   h   i   j   k   l

(**g**) FRANKFORT-ON-MAIN, Germany. Fayence. Est. 1666. (**h**) LONGTON, Great Britain. Circa 1750. (**i**) BOW, Great Britain. Porcelain. Circa 1760. (**j**) MOUSTIERS, France. Hard paste and soft paste. Circa 1775. (**k**) MOUSTIERS, France. Fayence. Circa 1775. (**l**) BOW, Great Britain. Thomas Frye. Porcelain. 1744.

m   n   o   p   q

(**m**) MARSEILLES, France. Joseph Fauchier II. Fayence. 17th and 18th centuries. (**n**) BOW, Great Britain. Est. 1750-1760. (**o**) COPENHAGEN, Denmark. Jacob Fortling. Fayence. 1755-1762. (**p**) BERNBURG, Germany. Fayence. 1725. (**q**) COPENHAGEN, Denmark. Fournier. Soft paste. Painted blue. 1759-1765.

a   b   c   d   e

(a) HOLLAND. F. M. Byckloh. Fayence. Delft. 1680. (b) GREIN-STADT, Germany. Franz Baroto. Circa 1850. (c) PARIS, France. Francois Briat. Fayence. Circa 1600. (d) LILLE, France. Francois Boussemart. Fayence. Circa 1750. (e) LILLE, France. Fràncois Boussemart. Circa 1750.

FBB   FBF   *ℬℒ* F^d f^d

f   g   h   i   j

(f) WORCESTER, Great Britain. Flight, Barr, and Barr. 1813-1840. (g) FAENZA, Italy. Fayence. 18th century. (h) MOUS-TIERS, France. Joseph Olery. Fayence. 18th century. (i) MOUS-TIERS, France. Pottery. Painted. 1780. (j) MOUSTIERS, France. Fayence. 18th century.

F D V N   F.e   Fer.   F.F. D.   F.G. 73

k   l   m   n   o

(k) NAPLES, Italy. 18th-19th century. (l) MOUSTIERS, France. Fayence. 18th century. (m) ALCORA, Spain. Fayence. 18th century. (n) DALLWITZ, Bohemia. Est. 1804. (o) ISLEWORTH, Great Britain. Joseph Shore. 1760.

ℍ   FHC   ﬖ   FLH   Ŧℰ

a   b   c   d   e

(a) ROUEN, France. 16th century. (b) HARRISBURG, Pennsylvania, U.S.A. Cowden and Wilcox. Impressed. Circa 1880. (c) MOUSTIERS, France. Fayence. 18th century. (d) FLORSHEIM, Germany. Fayence. Est. 1765. (e) MOUSTIERS, France. Joseph Olery. Fayence. 18th century.

F&M   Fo   F·P   FPC/F   F.R

f   g   h.   i   j

(f) PIRKENHAMMER, Bohemia. Hard paste. 1815-1845. (g) ALCORA, Spain. Fayence. Est. 1727. (h) MOUSTIERS, France. Fayence. 18th century. (i) FRANKLIN, Ohio, U.S.A. Franklin Pottery Company. Impressed. Circa 1880. (j) NEVERS, France. Pottery. Painted. 1730.

F·R⸱   F&R   (⁺⁺F⸱R   ·F.R.1734

k   l   m   n

(k) RATO, Portugal. Fayence. Est. 1767. (l) PIRKENHAMMER, Germany. Fischer and Reichembach. Hard paste. Painted. 1802. (m) PIRKENHAMMER, Germany. Fischer and Reichembach. Hard paste. 1802. (n) NEVERS, France. Fayence, 1734.

a   b   c

(a) DALLWITZ, Bohemia. 1845. (b) BUEN RETIRO, Spain. Soft paste. 1759. (c) PESARO, Italy. Circa 1870.

d   e   f

(d) ALCORA, Spain. Fayence. Est. 1727. (e) PARIS, France. Pont-aux-Choux. 1794. (f) SAINT VERAIN, France. 1764.

g   h   i

(g) ROUEN, France. Fayence. 1644. (h) MARTRES, France. Fayence. 1775. (i) LILLE, France. Porcelain. 19th century.

1789
fait Par Pierre
a mony
F. and R. PRATT & Co.
FENTON

Fatto cn Torino

a   b   c

(a) ROUEN, France. Fayence. 1789. (b) FENTON, Great Britain.
F. and R. Pratt and Company. Pottery. After 1810. (c) TURIN,
Italy. Fayence. 16th century.

FENTON & HANCOCK
ST. JOHNSBURY
FELL   **FELL & Co.**   **FENIX**   VT.

d   e   f   g

(d-e) NEWCASTLE-ON-TYNE, Great Britain. Thomas Fell, potter, 18th-19th century. (f) EAST LIVERPOOL, Ohio, U.S.A. Smith-
Phillips China Company. 19th century. (g) ST. JOHNSBURY, Vermont, U.S.A. Fenton and Hancock, Impressed. Circa 1870.

FENTON STONE WORKS
C. J. M. & Co.
ferrat moustiers
FERRYBRIDGE

h   i   j

(h) FENTON, Great Britain. Charles J. Mason and Company. Before 1856. (i) MOUSTIERS, France. Fayence. 1760. (j) FERRY-
BRIDGE, Great Britain. Pottery. Est. 1792.

F. F.

a   b   c

(a) PARIS, France. Hard paste. Painted red. 1790. (b) VENEZIA, Italy. Treviso. 1799. (c) MOUSTIERS, France. Fayence. 1745.

d   e   f   g

(d) HARRISBURG. Pennsylvania, U.S.A. Cowden and Wilcox. 1880. (e) HUNTINGTON, New York, U.S.A. Frederick J. Caire. Circa 1860. (f) SHELTON, Great Britain. Circa 1786. (g) PARIS, France. M. F. Fleury. 1773.

Flight   *FLIGHTS*   *Flight Barr & Barr*

h   i   j

(h) WORCESTER, Great Britain. Blue. 1782-1791. (i) WORCESTER, Great Britain. 1782-1791. (j) WORCESTER, Great Britain. 1813-1840.

a   b   c

(a) WORCESTER, Great Britain. Flight and Barr. 1792-1807. (b) Rotterdam, Holland. 1812. (c) PARIS, France. Porcelain. 1785-1820.

FOLEY

E. BRAIN & CO., LTD.   FORD   Ford Pottery, South Hylton   x Fortuÿn

d   e   f   g

(d) STOKE-ON-TRENT, Great Britain. E. Brain and Company. Foley China. 20th century. (e-f) SUNDERLAND, Great Britain. Ford Pottery Company. Est. 1800. (g) HOLLAND. De Fortuyn (The Fortune). Pieter van der Briel. Fayence. Delft. Painted blue. 1691.

Fossé   FOWLER, THOMPSON & Co.   FULPER BROS FLEMINGTON, N.J.   FREDERICK MEAR

h   i   j   k

(h) ROUEN, France. 16th century. (i) PRESTONPANS, Scotland. Fowler, Thompson, and Company. Circa 1825. (j) BOSTON, Massachusetts, U.S.A. Frederick Mear. Impressed. Circa 1840. (k) FLEMINGTON, New Jersey, U.S.A. Fulper Brothers. Impressed. After 1805.

a   b   c   d   e   f

SECTION G
See also Sections
C, Lines

(a) BOW, Great Britain. Porcelain. 1744-1776. (b) BUEN RE-
TIRO, Spain. Soft paste. 1759-1808. (c-d) GOTHA, Germany.
Painted blue. 1805-1830. (e) ST. PETERSBURG, Russia. Blue.
Circa 1760. (f) TAVERNES, France. Fayence. 1760-1780.

g   h   i   j   k   l

(g) FAENZA, Italy. Fayence. 15th century. (h) TAVERNES,
France. Fayence. 1760-1780. (i) TOURNAY, Belgium. Boch Brothers. 1850. (j) MOUSTIERS, France. Joseph Olery. Fayence. 18th
century. (k) MOUSTIERS, France. Fayence. 18th century. (l)
GOTHA, Germany. Hard paste. Painted blue. Est. 1757.

m   n   o   p   q   r

(m-n) GERA, Germany. Hard paste. Painted blue. 1780. (o) BOW,
Great Britain. Porcelain. 1750-1770. (p) BERLIN, Germany. Gotz-
kowsky. 1761-1763. (q) ST. PETERSBURG, Russia. Painted blue.
Circa 1758. (r) NYON, Switzerland. Porcelain. 1780.

a   b   c   d   e

(a) TAVERNES, France. Fayence. 1760-1780. (b) PARIS, France.
Dihl and Guerhard. Duc d'Angouleme, patron. Hard paste. Painted
red. 1780. (c) ROUEN, France. Guillebaud. 1730. (d) HOLLAND.
De Lampetkan (The Ewer). G. Brouwer. Fayence. 1756. (e)
RENNES, France. Est. 18th century.

f   g   h   i   j

(f) HOLLAND. De Dubbelde Schenkkan (The Double Jug). Fayence. Delft. 1721. (g) LIMOGES, France. 1842-1898. (h) WIN-
TERTHUR, Switzerland. Fayence. 1655. (i) NAPLES, Italy. Guis-
tini Brothers. 18th century. (j) BUEN RETIRO, Spain. Soft paste.
1759-1808.

k   l   m   n   o

(k) WINTERTHUR, Switzerland. Pfaum. 1688. (l) HOLLAND.
Fayence. Delft. Painted. Circa 1700. (m) PARIS, France. Guy and
Housel, potters. Late 18th and early 19th centuries. (n) HOLLAND.
De Dubbelde Schenkkan. (The Double Jug). Fayence. Delft. 1721.
(o) STRASBURG, France. Joseph Hannong. Circa 1771.

G.L
G
1728
K . 30 Dec: ₣℘
+....
G PS
176£ .
G. R. 1651

a   b   c   d   e

(a) HOLLAND. De Griekse A (The Greek A). G. L. Kruyk.
Fayence. Delft. 1645. (b) MEISSEN, Germany. Hard paste. 1728.
(c) MOUSTIERS, France. Joseph Olery. Fayence. 18th century.
(d) HOLLAND. De Porceleyne Schootel (The Porcelain Dish).
Fayence. Delft. 1764. (e) WROTHAM, Great Britain. 1651.

GVJ   ₣:v :.ς   GALLOWAY &GRAFF
PHILADELPHIA   ςardin

f   g   h   i

(f) HOLLAND. De Oude Moriaan's Hooft (The Old Moor's
Head). Fayence. Delft. Painted blue. 1764. (g) HOLLAND. De
Oude Moriaan's Hooft (The Old Moor's Head). Fayence. Delft.
1764. (h) PHILADELPHIA, Pennsylvania, U.S.A. Galloway and
Graff. Est. 1868. (i) ROUEN, France. Nicolas Gardin. 1760.

GARNKIRK   G
BAYEUX   G. BENTON
&
L. STEWART
HARTFORD   ςDa
FRANCE

j   k   l   m

(j) SCOTLAND, Garnkirk Company. Circa 1870. (k) BAYEUX,
France. F. Gosse, proprietor. 1849. (l) HARTFORD, Connecticut,
U.S.A. G. Benton and L. Stewart. Circa 1818. (m) LIMOGES,
France. 1842-1898.

Genève   G.E.OHR   George Grainger.   Gera
             BILOXI   Royal China Works,
                            Worcester.

a   b   c   d

(a) NYON, Switzerland. Porcelain. 1781-1813. (b) EAST BILOXI,
Mississippi, U.S.A. George Ohr. Circa 1900. (c) WORCESTER,
Great Britain. Porcelain. Circa 1830. (d) GERA, Germany. Blue
underglaze. Est. 1779.

                          C.G.
                          pesaro
G. F. BOWERS   1705   G.H.&CO.   G.H.Kittredge.

e   f   g   h

(e) TUNSTALL, Great Britain, G. F. Bowers. Circa 1850. (f)
PESARO, Italy. 1765. (g) SWANSEA, Wales. 1765-1870. (h)
TRENTON, New Jersey, U.S.A. Glasgow Pottery Company. Circa
1875.

Gide 1789   GEISSHÜBEL   Giordano   GINORI

i   j   k   l

(i) NYON, Switzerland. Porcelain. 1789. (j) GIESSHUBEL, Germany. Porcelain. Circa 1815. (k) NAPLES, Italy. Michele Giordano
and son, modelers. Late 18th and early 19th centuries. (l) DOCCIA,
Italy. Soft paste. Impressed. 1821.

Giuseppe Fumo   GLASCOW   GLASGOW CHINA VITRIFIED TRENTON N J   *G. Manjack fecit* PROSKAU

a   b   c   d

(a) BUEN RETIRO, Spain. Guiseppe Fumo, modeler. Soft paste. 1759-1808. (b-c) TRENTON, New Jersey, U.S.A. Glasgow Pottery Company. Circa 1875. (d) PROSKAU, Germany. Fayence. 1817.

göggingen H S   GOODALE + STEDMAN HARTFORD 1822   GOODWIN & WEBSTER

e   f   g

(e) GOGGINGEN, Germany. Fayence. H. Simon, painter. Est. 1748. (f) HARTFORD, Connecticut, U.S.A. Goodale and Stedman. 1822. (g) HARTFORD, Connecticut, U.S.A. Goodwin and Webster. Circa 1825.

GOODWIN'S HOTEL CHINA   *Gotha.*   G.P. Co.   *Grainger, Lee & Co.*

h   i   j   k

(h) LIVERPOOL, Ohio, U.S.A. John Goodwin. Stoneware. Circa 1850. (i) GOTHA, Germany. Circa 1805. (j) TRENTON, New Jersey, U.S.A. Greenwood Pottery. Printed. Est. 1864. (k) WORCESTER, Great Britain. Hard paste. Painted red. 1800.

GRAINGER, WOOD & CO.   **GREEN**
   WORCESTER,   **GREEN**   **DON POTTERY**   GREEN,
   WARRENTED   LEEDS

a   b   c   d

(a) WORCESTER, Great Britain. Porcelain. 1800. (b) LIVER-
POOL, Great Britain. Guy Green. Late 18th century. (c) SWIN-
TON, Great Britain. Don Pottery. 1790. (d) LEEDS, Great Britain.
Circa 1760.

                    GREENWOOD CHINA   GREENWOOD
GREEN, LIVERPOOL   TRENTON, N.J.   POTTERY   GR et Cⁱᵉ

        e   f   g   h

(e) LIVERPOOL, Great Britain. Guy Green. Late 18th century.
(f-g) TRENTON, New Jersey. U.S.A. Greenwood Pottery Company. Printed. Circa 1870. (h) LIMOGES, France. Circa 1773.

𝒢 roft 'my   GROS   GROSVENOR & SON   GRUEBY

     i   j   k   l

(i) ISLE ST. DENIS, France. Porcelain. Est. 1778. (j) ALCORA,
Spain. Fayence, porcelain. Est. 1750. (k) SCOTLAND. Grosvenor
and Son. Circa 1870. (l) BOSTON, Massachusetts, U.S.A. Grueby
Faience Company, Est. 1897.

a   b   c   d

(**a**) GREAT BRITAIN. Wincanton Pottery. 1737. (**b**) PARIS, France. Hard paste. Stenciled red. 1780. (**c**) ROUEN, France. Guillibaud, potter. 1720-1750. (**d**) HOLLAND. Gysbert Verhaast. Fayence. Delft. Circa 1760.

Section **H**
See also Section
Lines

e   f   g   h   i   j

(**e**) PARIS, France. 18th century. (**f**) FAUBOURG ST. LAZARE, France. Hannong. Porcelain. 1773. (**g**) STRASBURG, Germany. Fayence, porcelain. Circa 1750. (**h**) STRASBURG, Germany. Pierre Hannong. Fayence. Circa 1750. (**i**) PARIS, France. Hannong. Hard paste and pottery. Painted color. 1773. (**j**) HOLLAND. De Ster (The Star). D. Hofdick. Fayence. Delft. 1705.

k   l   m   n   o

(**k**) STRASBURG, Germany. J. Hannong. Hard paste and pottery. Painted blue. 1752. (**l**) ALT-ROHLAU, Bohemia. Benedict Hasslacher, proprietor. 1813-1823. (**m**) NEVERS, France. Fayence. 17th century. (**n-o**) STRASBURG, Germany. Joseph Hannong. Fayence, porcelain. 1752.

| a | b | c | d | e |

(**a**) HOLLAND. De Drie Porceleyne Fleschen (The Three Porcelain Bottles). Hugo Brouwer. Fayence. Delft. Painted blue. 1764.
(**b**) HOLLAND. De Drie Porceleyne Fleschen (The Three Porcelain Bottles). Hugo Brouwer. Fayence. Delft. 1764. (**c**) QUIMPER, France. Antoine de la Hubaudiere. 1782. (**d**) NEVERS, France. Henri Borne. Fayence. Painted color. 1680. (**e**) HERREBOE, Norway. Hosenfeller. 1762.

| f | g | h | i | j |

(**f**) GOULT, France. Fayence. Est. 1740. (**g**) SWITZERLAND. Fayence. 1634. (**h**) PARIS, France. Fayence. Circa 1850. (**i**) TURIN, Italy. Fayence. 18th century. (**j**) HOLLAND. Fayence. Delft. 17th century.

| k | l | m | n | o |

(**k**) HOLLAND. De Dubbelde Schenkkan (The Double Jug). Fayence. 1721. (**l**) WINTERTHUR, Switzerland. Fayence. 1607. (**m**) VINCENNES, France. Hannong and Laborde. Porcelain. 1765. (**n**) NAPLES, Italy. 18th century. (**o**) WINTERTHUR, Switzerland. Fayence. 17th century.

Ħ.I /669   M ℛ   **Ħ𝕂**   ĦK   ⊦K

a   b   c   d   e

(a) WROTHAM, Great Britain. Slipware. 1669. (b) STRASBURG, Germany. J. and P. Hannong. Fayence, hard paste. Painted blue. 1700. (c) STRASBURG, Germany. Hannong. Fayence, hard paste. 18th century. (d) HOLLAND. Jan Zoon Kuylich. Fayence. Delft. 1680. (e) PRAGUE, Germany. Prager. Porcelain. 1810-1835.

HKL   𝐻𝐿   ⊦L   𝐻𝐿·   hℓℓ

f   g   h   i   j

(f) HERREBOE, Norway. Peter Hofnagel, founder. Fayence. 1762. (g) STRASBURG, Germany. Hannong. Fayence, porcelain. 18th century. (h) HOLLAND. De Porceleyne Fles (The Porcelain Bottle). J. Harlees. 1770. (i) VINCENNES, France. Hard paste. 1764. (j) VINCENNES, France. Hannong and Laborde. Hard paste. 1765.

)M   ƷP   FP   Ħ.P.   *H P* /6) 6

k   l   m   n   o

(k) ZANESVILLE, Ohio, U.S.A. American Encaustic Tiling Company. 19th century. (l) PARIS, France. Fayence. 1862. (m) BRUGES, Flanders. Fayence. Est. 1751. (n) HANLEY, Great Britain. Humphrey Palmer, potter. Staffordshire. 1760. (o) WINTERTHUR, Switzerland. Fayence. 17th century.

a　　　　　b　　　　　c　　　　　d

(a) MONTGOMERY, Pennsylvania, U.S.A. Henry Roudebuth. 19th century. (b) MORRISVILLE, Pennsylvania, U.S.A. Robertson Tile Company. 19th century. (c) STRASBURG, France. Hannong. Fayence, hard paste. Painted blue. 1709. (d) HOLLAND. F. v. Hesse. Fayence. 1730.

e　　　　　f　　　　　g　　　　　h

(e) HOLLAND. De Roos (The Rose). Fayence. Delft. 1732. (f) DERBY, Great Britain. H. S. Keys, painter. Hard paste. Late 18th– early 19th century. (g) STRASBURG, France. Hannong. Fayence, porcelain. 1709. (h) Holland. De Roos (The Rose). H. v. d. Bosch. 1803.

i　　　　　j　　　　　k　　　　　l　　　　　m

(i) HOLLAND. Fayence. Delft. Painted blue. Hendrick Van Hoorn. 1764. (j) HOLLAND. T'Hart (The Stag). Hendrick van Middeldijk. 1764. (k) STRASBURG, France. Hannong. Fayence, porcelain. 1709. (l) PARIS, France. Samson, the imitator. Circa 1875. (m) VINCENNES, France. Hard paste. 1800.

Haas & Czjzek
in
Schlaggenwald   *Hackwood*   HACKWOOD & CO.

a   b   c

(a) SCHLAGGENWALD, Germany. Porcelain. 1840. (b) SHEL-
TON, Great Britain. Fayence. Impressed. 1842. (c) SHELTON,
Great Britain. 1842.

HADDONFIELD, N.J.   Haidinger   halley
C. W. & BRO.

d   e   f

(d) HADDONFIELD, New Jersey, U.S.A. Charles Wingender and
brother. Impressed. Circa 1890. (e) ELBOGEN, Germany. Earthenware, porcelain. 1815. (f) PARIS, France. Halley, decorator. Early
19th century.

HAMILTON & JONES   HAMPSHIRE   H&C°   H&C°
GREENSBORO, PA.   POTTERY

g   h   i   j

(g) GREENSBORO, Pennsylvania, U.S.A. Hamilton and Jones.
Impressed. Circa 1870. (h) KEENE, New Hampshire, U.S.A.
Hampshire Pottery Company. Painted red. Circa 1875. (i) HAVI-
LAND, France. Whiteware for presidential sets. Painted green.
Circa 1879. (j) HAVILAND, France. Whiteware. Painted green.
Circa 1880.

H&C°   H&C°   H&C°   H&C°   [HANLEY E⊞D ENGLAND]
         DEPOSE   L   L
                             FRANCE

a   b   c   d   e

(a) HAVILAND, France. Whiteware. Painted green. Circa 1880.
(b) HAVILAND, France. Whiteware. Painted green. 1887. (c)
HAVILAND, France. Painted red, black, blue or green on decorated
ware; painted green on whiteware. 1876. (d) HAVILAND, France.
Whiteware. Painted green. 1891. (e) HANLEY, Great Britain.
E. J. Bodley. Late 19th century.

HARDMUTH   Horley   HARTLEY, GREEN & CO.

f   g   h

(f) BUDWEIS, Germany. Carl Hardmuth. Porcelain. 1846. (g)
LANE END, Great Britain. Pottery and hard paste. Impressed.
1809. (h) LEEDS, Great Britain. Pottery. Est. 1750.

HARTLEY GREEN & CO.   [HARTLEY GREENS POTTERY CO]   HASTINGS & BELDING
LEEDS POTTERY   ASHFIELD
                                                        MASS.

i   j   k

(i) LEEDS, Great Britain. Est. 1750. (j) LEEDS, Great Britain.
Pottery. Est. 1750. (k)ASHFIELD, Massachusetts, U.S.A. Hastings
and Belding. Impressed. Circa 1855.

HAVILAND&CO.   Haviland & Co. Limoges   Haviland's Ghantilly

a   b   c

(a) HAVILAND, France. Decorated ware. Painted red, green, black, blue. 1876. (b) HAVILAND, France. Red. 1889. (c) HAVI-LAND, France. Decorated ware. Painted red and green. 1948-1953.

Haviland France   HAWLEY   HAXTUN & CO. FORT EDWARD N.Y.   HAYNES DILLWYN & C? CAMBRIAN POTTERY SWANSEA

d   e   f   g

(d) HAVILAND, France. Whiteware. Painted green. 1893. (e) LEEDS, Great Britain. Hawley, potter. Kilnhurst. 1800. (f) FORT EDWARD, New York, U.S.A. Haxton and Company. Impressed. Circa 1875. (g) SWANSEA, Wales. 1790-1802.

H. BOOTH   H. CANS   H&C? L FRANCE   Heath

h   i   j   k

(h) STOKE-ON-TRENT, Great Britain. Hugo Booth. Circa 1785. (i) LANCASTER, Pennsylvania, U.S.A. H. Gans. Circa 1870. (j) LIMOGES, France. Est. 1840. (k) DERBY, Great Britain. Pottery. Impressed. 1760.

Heindering Waanders
1781   HELEN   HELSINBERG

a   b   c

(a) HOLLAND. H. Waanders. Fayence. Delft. 1781. (b) EVANS-
VILLE, Indiana, U.S.A. Crown Pottery Company. Est. 1891. (c)
HELSINBERG, Sweden. 1770.

HENDERSON'S FLINT
STONEWARE   HENRI   HENRY LEWIS
MANUFACTORY   DEUX

d   e   f

(d) JERSEY CITY, New Jersey, U.S.A. Jersey City Pottery Com-
pany. 1830. (e) ZANESVILLE, Ohio, U.S.A. J. B. Owens Pottery
Company. Circa 1890. (f) HUNTINGTON, New Hampshire,
U.S.A. Impressed. Circa 1825.

Henry Roudebuth
April || 28ᵗʰ 1811
                                              H. H. MELLICK
                                              ROSEVILLE
                HERCULANEUM   HEREND   OHIO

g   h   i   j

(g) MONTGOMERY, Pennsylvania, U.S.A. Henry Roudebuth.
19th century. (h) LIVERPOOL, Great Britain. Pottery. Impressed.
1796. (i) HEREND, Hungary. Moritz Fischer. Hard paste. Painted
blue. After 1839. (j) ROSEVILLE, Ohio, U.S.A. H. H. Mellick.
Impressed. Circa 1875.

HICKS & MEIGH   HIRAM SWANK & SONS JOHNSTOWN, PA.   HOBSON   HOLLITSCH

a   b   c   d

(a) SHELTON, Great Britain. Hicks and Meigh. 1806-1820. (b) JOHNSTOWN, Pennsylvania, U.S.A. Hiram Swank and Sons. Impressed. Circa 1875. (c) EVANSVILLE, Indiana, U.S.A. Crown Pottery Company. Est. 1891. (d) HOLLITSCH, Hungary. Impressed. Circa 1800.

Hooren   HOTEL GP CO.   HOTEL V. P. Co.   Housel   H & R DANIEL

e   f   g   h   i

(e) HOLLAND, De Drie Porceleyne Astonnen (The Three Porcelain Ash Barrels). Fayence. Delft. Painted blue. 1764. (f) EAST LIVERPOOL, Ohio, U.S.A. Globe Pottery Company. Est. 1888. (g) EAST LIVERPOOL, Ohio, U.S.A. Vodrey Brothers. Circa 1875. (h) PARIS, France. Hard paste. Painted. 1799. (i) STOKE-ON-TRENT, Great Britain. Circa 1830.

H. Stofflet   H V'hvorn   H. WORES   DAVETJN

j   k   l.   m

(j) BERKS, Pennsylvania, U.S.A. Heinrich Stofflet. Circa 1815. (k) Holland, De Drie Astonnen (The Three Ash Barrels). H. V. Hoorn. Fayence. Delft. 1759. (l) DOVER, Ohio, U.S.A. H. Wores. Impressed. Circa 1830. (m) HOLLAND. H. Zieremans. Fayence. Delft. 1757.

a   b   c   d   e   f

(a) ALTHALDENSLEBEN, Germany. Hard paste. Impressed.
1810. (b) ILMENAU, Germany. Porcelain. Est. 1777. (c) BOW,
Great Britain. Painted red, blue. Est. 1744. (d) ST. CLOUD,
France. Fayence, porcelain. 1678-1766. (e) LISBON, Portugal. Est.
1773. (f) BRISTOL, Great Britain. Painted blue, gold. 18th century.

iB   ₿   I.C.   I. D.   i DA

g   h   i   j   k

(g) HOLLAND. De Ster (The Star). Fayence. Delft. Painted blue.
1764. (h) HOLLAND. De Porceleyne Byl (The Porcelain Hatchet).
J. Brouwer. 1759. (i) NEW YORK, New York, U.S.A. John Crolius.
Impressed. Circa 1790. (j) PARIS, France. M. J. Devers. Fayence.
1850. (k) HOLLAND. De Vergulde Boot (The Golden Boat). Johannes der Appel. Fayence. Delft. 1764.

I.D.M   ID w   I.E. 1697   I.E.B.   IG 1709

l   m   n   o   p

(l) HOLLAND. De Paauw (The Peacock). Jacobus de Milde. Fayence. Delft. 1764. (m) HOLLAND. J. d. Weert. Fayence. Delft.
1663. (n) WROTHAM, Great Britain. Slipware. 17th and 18th centuries. (o) SHELTON, Great Britain. Ralph and John Baddeley.
Circa 1772. (p) WINTERTHUR, Switzerland. Pfau. 17th century.

H a   I.H. 1764 b   I.H.D c   *IK* d   İ K e

(a) STRASBURG, France. Paul Hannong. 1752. (b) WORCES-
TER, Great Britain. 1764. (c) HOLLAND. Fayence. Delft. Painted
blue. 1765. (d) MORTLAKE, Great Britain. Late 18th century.
(e) HOLLAND. De Oude Moriaan's Hooft (The Old Moor's
Head). J. Kool. 1676.

I K f   *IK* g   *I☆K* h   I.L. 1638 i $\frac{ITD}{7}$ j

(f) HOLLAND, De Dubbelde Schenkkan (The Double Jug). 1714.
(g) HOLLAND. Jan Kuylich, the younger. Fayence. Delft. Painted
blue. 1680. (h) HOLLAND. Jan Kuylich. Fayence. Delft. Painted
blue. 1680. (i) WROTHAM, Great Britain. 17th century. (j) HOL-
LAND. De Griekse A (The Greek A). J. T. Dextra. Fayence. Delft.
1764.

$\frac{ITD}{12}$ k $\frac{ITD}{DEX}$ // l   **I V** m   IVH 1728 n   I V K o

(k) HOLLAND. De Griekse A (The Greek A). J. T. Dextra. Fayence. Delft. 1764. (l) HOLLAND. De Griekse A (The Greek A).
1764. (m) HOLLAND. De Fortuyn (The Fortune). Fayence.
Delft. 1691. (n) HOLLAND. De Jonge Moriaan's Hooft (The New
Moor's Head). Fayence. Delft. 1728. (o) HOLLAND. De Drie
Astonnen (The Three Ash Barrels). J. P. v. Kessel. Fayence. Delft.
1655.

I Y Þ ᴧ C   I.V J   I V V   I.W

a   b   c   d

(a) HOLLAND. De Klauw (The Claw). J. Van Putten and Com-
pany. Fayence. Delft. 1830-1850. (b) HOLLAND. De Oude
Moriaan's Hooft (The Old Moor's Head). G. Verstelle. Fayence.
Delft. 1764. (c) HOLLAND. De Oude Moriaan's Hooft (The Old
Moor's Head). 1661. (d) WROTHAM, Great Britain. Slipware.
17th-18th century.

J·A a l m i ᵴ·P   I. B. FARRAR & SONS   I. CYPLES

        e   f   g

(e) ROTTERDAM, Holland. Pieter Janz Aelmis, potter. Fayence.
1691-1707. (f) FAIRFAX, Vermont, U.S.A. Isaac Farrar. Circa 1800.
(g) LANE END, Great Britain. Cyples, potter. Staffordshire. Late
18th-early 19th century.

I. DALE   I E: W: 1699:
BURSLEM   WROT:HAM   I Hall & Sons   I. H. WANDS

   h   i   j   k

(h) BURSLEM, Great Britain. J. Dale, potter. Staffordshire. Late
18th-early 19th cenutry. (i) WROTHAM, Great Britain. Slipware.
1699. (j) GREAT BRITAIN. John Hall and Sons. Staffordshire.
Circa 1810. (k) OLEANS, New York, U.S.A. I. H. Wands. Impressed. Circa 1860.

İn ˙ DE - OELF
SE . VIN - KEL.
I. MEAD   ;T.D.   INDIAN CHINA   INTERNATIONAL CHINA TRENTON N J

a   b   c·   d

(a) ATWATER, Ohio, U.S.A. I. Mead and Company. Impressed.
Circa 1850. (b) HOLLAND. De Dessel (The Axe). Fayence. Delft.
1696. (c) TRENTON, New Jersey, U.S.A. Ceramic Art Company.
Est. 1879. (d) TRENTON, New Jersey, U.S.A. Burgess and Campbell. Est. 1879.

I Perdv   I P.S   IRONSTONE   CHINA
1734   A LYON   BURGESS & CAMPELL
                 1773

e   f   g

(e) ROUEN, France. J. Perdu, painter. 1734-1756. (f) LYONS,
France. Fayence. 1773. (g) TRENTON, New Jersey, U.S.A. Burgess
and Campbell. Est. 1879.

ISAAC HEWETT
EXCELSIOR WORKS
PRICES LANDING
I· R· Palvdev·   PENNA.   I. Smith

h   i   j

(h) NANTES, France. Fayence. 1634. (i) PRICE'S LANDING,
Pennsylvania, U.S.A. Isaac Hewitt. Painted blue. Circa 1875. (j)
WRIGHTSTOWN, Pennsylvania, U.S.A. Joseph Smith. Circa 1775.

a   b   c   d   e

(a) WINCANTON, Great Britian. Nathaniel Ireson. potter. 1740-1750. (b) HANLEY, Great Britain. Job Ridgway, owner. 1802. (c) BURSLEM, Great Britain. Bagshaw and Maier. Circa 1800. (d) GREAT BRITAIN. Old Hall Works. Earthenware. Est. 1790. (e) TROY, New York, U.S.A. Israel Seymour. Impressed. Circa 1825.

SECTION J
See also Sections
L, Lines

f   g   h   i   j

(f) THURINGIA, Germany. Ilmenau. Fayence, porcelain. Est. 1777. (g) LONGTON, Great Britain. William Littler, potter. Porcelain, stoneware. 1750-1760. (h) APREY, France. Fayence. Est. 1750. (i) LA ROCHELLE, France. J. Briqueville. Est. 1743. (j) HOLLAND. De Boot (The Boot) J. d. Appel. Fayence. 1759.

k   l   m   n   o   p

(k) HANLEY, Great Britain. J. Dimmock and Company. Late 19th century. (l) KREUSSEN, Germany. Caspar and H. C. Vest. Stoneware. Painted color. Circa 1623. (m) Holland. Jan Gaal, potter. 1707-1725. (n) STOKE-ON-TRENT, Great Britain. G. Jones and Sons. Late 19th-early 20th century. (o) STRASBURG, France. P. Hannong. Fayence, porcelain. 1709-1780. (p) WORCESTER, Great Britain. James Hadley and Sons. Porcelain. 1896-1903.

a   b   c   d   e

(a) SOUTH AMBOY. New Jersey, U.S.A. Warns and Letts. Circa 1805. (b) COTE-D'OR, France. Premieres, factory. Fayence. Stenciled blue. 19th century. (c) MOUSTIERS, France. Joseph Olery. Fayence. 18th century. (d) HOLLAND. De Fortuyn (The Fortune). Fayence. Delft. 1706. (e) AUSSIG, Bohemia. Jon Maresch. 1840.

f   g   h   i   j

(f) ST. CLOUD, France. Soft paste. 1678-1766. (g) FONTAINE-BLEAU, France. Jacob Petit, potter. Hard paste. Painted blue. Circa 1800. (h) LIMOGES, France. J. Pouyat, potter. Painted red. 1842. (i) NEW YORK, New York, U.S.A. John Remney. Stoneware. Circa 1775. (j) MARSEILLES, France. Joseph Robert, potter. Porcelain. 1754-1793. .

k   l   m   n   o

(k) LIONVILLE, Pennsylvania, U.S.A. J. Vickers. Circa 1805. (l) HOLLAND. De Griekse A (The Greek A). Fayence, Delft. 1701. (m) WEISBADEN, Germany. Circa 1780. (n) BURTON-ON TRENT, Great Britain. Ashby Potter's Guild. Pottery. Est. 1909. (o) POUGHKEEPSIE, New York, U.S.A. Jacob Caire. Impressed. Circa 1850.

JACOB DICK
TUSCARAWAS CO.   Jacob Medinger   Jacob Taney
OHIO

a   b   c

(a) TUSCARAWAS COUNTY, Ohio, U.S.A. Jacob Dick. Impressed. 1835. (b) NEIFFER, Pennsylvania, U.S.A. Jacob Medinger. Circa 1885-1930. (c) NOCKAMIXON, Pennsylvania, U.S.A. Jacob Taney. Circa 1795.

J Albany f.   JAMES HAMILTON
                     GREENSBORO, PA.
                                              J. BELL

d   e   f

(d) CASTILLE, Spain. Talavera de la Reyna, factory. Fayence. 17th-18th century. (e) GREENSBORO, Pennsylvania, U.S.A. James Hamilton. Impressed. Circa 1875. (f) WAYNESBORO, Pennsylvania, U.S.A. John Bell. Impressed. Circa 1875.

J. & E. NORTON & CO.
BENNINGTON, VT   J.A.Weber   J.BENNETT N.Y.

g   h   i

(g) BENNINGTON, Vermont, U.S.A. J. and E. Norton. Impressed. Circa 1855. (h) BARNESVILLE, Pennsylvania, U.S.A. J. A. Wever. Impressed. Circa 1875. (i) NEW YORK, New York, U.S.A. John Bennett. Circa 1875.

a   b   c   d

(a) MOULTONBORO, New Hampshire, U.S.A. James S. Bennett. Impressed. Circa 1842. (b) NEVERS, France. J. Boulard, potter. Fayence. 1622. (c) DENBY, Great Britain. J. Bourne, potter. 19th century. (d) TUSCARAWAS COUNTY, Ohio, U.S.A. Jacob Dick. Impressed. 1835.

e   f   g   h

(e) NEVERS. France. Pierre Custode, potter. Fayence. 1632-1656. (f) FENTON, Great Britain. J. Edwards and Son. Circa 1875. (g) MORGANTOWN, Pennsylvania, U.S.A. Jesse Klugh. 1874. (h) EVANSVILLE, Indiana, U.S.A. Crown Pottery Company. Circa 1900.

i   j   k   l

(i) KLUM, Bohemia. Feresch. Porcelain. 1835. (j) NEWPORT, Ohio, U.S.A. Joseph Figley. Impressed. Circa 1850. (k) HARTFORD, Connecticut, U.S.A. J. C. Fisher. Impressed. Circa 1810. (l) BURSLEM, Great Britain. J. Lockett, potter. Earthenware, saltglazed stoneware. 1802.

J & J G. LOW,
PATENT
ART TILE WORKS
CHELSEA
J. H. WEATHERBY MASS. U.S.A. J.K. CALLAND
& SONS COPYRIGHT 1881 BY J & J LOW (LANDON POTTERY)

a   b   c

(a) HANLEY, Great Britain. J. H. Weatherby and Sons. Stafford-shire. Circa 1890. (b) CHELSEA, Massachusetts, U.S.A. Low Art Tile Company. 1881. (c) SWANSEA, Great Britain. John F. Cal-land. Circa 1850.

J. Keeling   J. LOCKETT   J. LOCKETT & SONS

d   e   f

(d) HANLEY, Great Britain. J. Keeling. Pottery. Impressed. 1790. (e) BURSLEM, Great Britain. J. Lockett, potter. Earthenware, salt-glazed stoneware. 1800. (f) BURSLEM, Great Britain. J. Lockett, potter. Earthenware, salt-glazed stoneware. 1829.

J.M.MADDEN
RONDOUT
J. M. & S. Co.   N.Y.   J G M P. B & C?   J. MEIGH & SONS

g   h   i   j

(g) TRENTON, New Jersey. U.S.A. John Moses and Sons. Circa 1875. (h) RANDOUT, New York, U.S.A. J. M. Madden. Impressed. Circa 1870. (i) SCOTLAND. J. and M. P. Bell and Company. Circa 1845. (j) HANLEY, Great Britain. Job Meigh and Sons, potters. Staffordshire. Impressed. Late 18th and 19th centuries.

a   b   c

(a-b) BENNINGTON, Vermont, U.S.A. Julius Norton. Impressed.
Circa 1845. (c) BENNINGTON, Vermont, U.S.A. J. Norton and
Company. Circa 1860.

d   e   f   g

(d) TYLER'S PORT, Pennsylvania, U.S.A. Johannes Leman. Circa
1830. (e) DORSET, Vermont, U.S.A. Jonathan Fenton. Impressed.
Circa 1805. (f) WAYNESBORO, Pennsylvania, U.S.A. John W. Bell.
Circa 1890. (g) SCHUYLKILL COUNTY, Pennsylvania, U.S.A.
John Boyer. Circa 1810.

h   i   j   k

(h) SENECA COUNTY, Ohio, U.S.A. John Hopkins. Impressed.
Circa 1835. (i) RAHWAY, New Jersey, U.S.A. John Mann. Im-
pressed. Circa 1835. (j) ELIZABETH, New Jersey, U.S.A. John
Pruden. Impressed. Circa 1870. (k) HANLEY, Great Britain. John
Ridgway, pottery owner. Staffordshire. 1802.

John Rose & Co.
COLEBROOK·DALE   JOHN SANDERS   JOHN W. BELL   JOHN WRIGHT

a   b   c   d

(a) COALPORT, Great Britain. John Rose, factory founder. 1793-
1841. (b) CONNECTICUT, U.S.A. John Sanders. Circa 1815. (c)
WAYNESBORO, Pennsylvania, U.S.A. John W. Bell. Circa 1890.
(d) GREAT BRITAIN. Jon Wright, artist. Slipware. Circa 1707.

J. OLDFIELD   JOSEPH BELL   Joseph   Glass JOSEPH.GLASS.SY.H.GX

e   f   g   h

(e) BRAMPTON, Great Britain. J. Oldfield, potter. Brownware.
1810. (f) PUTNAM, Ohio, U.S.A. Joseph Bell. Impressed. Circa
1835. (g-h) HANLEY, Great Britain. Joseph Glass, potter. Slipware.
1703.

                JOSEPH MAYER   Jos. Hemphill
José GRICCI   & Co.   Joseph Nigg.   Phila.

i   j   k   l

(i) BUEN RETIRO, Spain. Guiseppe Gricci, modeler. Soft paste.
1745-1770. (j) HANLEY, Great Britain. Joseph Mayer and Company. 19th century. (k) VIENNA, Austria. Porcelain. 1800. (l)
PHILADELPHIA, Pennsylvania, U.S.A. Joseph Hemphill. Painted
red. Circa 1835.

J·Q F

1 8 3

JOSHUA H ᴱᴬᵀᴴ JOSIAH   WEDGWOOD J & P int Fortuyn

a   b   c   d

(a) DERBY, Great Britain. Joshua Heath, potter. Pottery. Impressed. 1760. (b) ETRURIA, Great Britain. Wedgwood, factory. Josiah Wedgwood, potter and founder. Circa 1780. (c) NEW-CASTLE-ON-TYNE, Great Britain. Jackson and Patterson. Pottery. Circa 1800. (d) HOLLAND. De Fortuyn (The Fortune). 1706.

J. P.

J. PHILLIPS   **L.**   *J. REMMEY*
HYLTON POTTERY   **FRANCE.** *JP.*   *MANHATTAN WELLS*
                                                          NEW YORK

e   f   g   h

(e) SUNDERLAND, Great Britain. John Phillips, potter. Late 18th-early 19th century. (f) LIMOGES, France. Jean Pouyat, potter. 1842-1898. (g) FONTAINEBLEAU, France. Jacob Petit, potter. Circa 1800. (h) NEW YORK, New York, U.S.A. John Remmey III. Brown stoneware. Impressed. Circa 1800.

J. Sadler,   *J.S. EBERLEY*   *J.S.T. & Co.*
LIVERPL.   *J.S. BENNETT*   *STRASBURG*   *KEENE N. H*
                                    VA.

i   j   k   l

(i) LIVERPOOL, Great Britain. John Sadler, engraver for transfer printing. 1756-1770. (j) MOULTONBORO, New Hampshire, U.S.A. James S. Bennett. Impressed. Circa 1840. (k) STRASBURG, Virginia, U.S.A. J. S. Eberley. Impressed. Circa 1900. (l) KEENE, New Hampshire, U.S.A. J. S. Taft and Company. Circa 1875.

Julius Norton   Julius Norton
Bennington   East Bennington
VT.   VT   *J VDriet Ferit*

   a   b   c

(**a-b**) BENNINGTON, Vermont, U.S.A. Julius Norton. Impressed.
Circa 1845. (**c**) ROTTERDAM, Holland. Fayence. 17th-18th century.

J. VOYEZ   **J. WALLEY's ware**   **J. W. R Stone China**   **J. & W. R.**

   d   e   f   g

(**d**) HANLEY, Great Britain. John Voyez, modeler. Circa 1790.
(**e**) COBRIDGE, Great Britain. J. Walley. 1795. (**f**) SHELTON,
Great Britain. Job Ridgways, owner. 1794-1802. (**g**) SHELTON,
Great Britain. Bell Works. Pottery. Printed. 1770-1854.

SECTION **K**
See also Section
Lines   K   K   K   *K*   *K*   k

         h   i   j   k   l   m

(**h**) KLOSTERLE, Bohemia. Porcelain, lead-glazed earthenware.
1794-1803. (**i**) HOLLAND. Jan Kuylich. Fayence. Delft. Painted
blue. 17th century. (**j**) HOLLAND. De Drie Porceleyne Fleschen
(The Three Porcelain Bottles). Fayence. Delft. 1676. (**k**) KIEL,
Germany. Fayence. Circa 1770. (**l**) HOLLAND. Jan Kuylich, the
younger. Fayence. Delft. Painted blue. Registered 1680. (**m**) HOL-
LAND. De Porceleyne Fles (The Porcelain Bottle). Fayence. Delft.
1698.

a   b   c   d   e   f

(a) HOLSTEIN, Germany. Kiel, factory. Fayence. Painted gold or color. 1770. (b) HOLSTEIN, Germany. Kiel, factory. J. Buchwald, director. Fayence. 1770. (c-d) HOLSTEIN, Germany. Kiel, factory. Fayence. Circa 1770. (e-f) HOLSTEIN, Germany. Kiel, factory. Johann Tannich, director. 1763-1768.

g   h   i   j   k

(g) ·HOLSTEIN, Germany. Kellinghusen, factory. Dr. Grauer, potter. Fayence. 1795-1820. (h) HOLSTEIN, Germany. Kellinghusen, factory. Fayence. Circa 1800. (i) MEISSEN, Germany. Konigliche Hof Conditorei Warschau. Hard paste. 18th century. (j) MEISSEN, Germany. Konigliche Hof Conditorei Warschau. Hard paste. Painted blue. 18th century. (k) MEISSEN, Germany. Konigliche Porzellan Manufaktur. Hard paste. Underglaze blue. Circa 1723.

l   m   n   o   p

(l) KRISTER, Germany. 19th century. (m) PHILADELPHIA, Pennsylvania, U.S.A. Kurlbaum and Schwartz. Impressed. Circa 1850. (n) HOLLAND. De Porceleyne Fles (The Porcelain Bottle). Fayence. Delft. 1698. (o) HOLLAND. De Klauw (The Claw). Fayence. Delft. 1750. (p) HOLLAND. Fayence. Delft. Painted blue. 1700.

Keeling Toft & Co.   Kenneth   KEZONTA

a   b   c

(a) HANLEY, Great Britain. Keeling, potter. Staffordshire. Impressed. 1806-1824. (b) FLEMINGTON, New Jersey, U.S.A. Fulper Brothers. Impressed. 19th century. (c) CINCINNATI, Ohio, U.S.A. Cincinnati Art Pottery Company. Est. 1879.

KIEBZ
K & G   13   KIEBƷ   Kiel
LUNEVILLE K. Herr II   15   Kiel   T

d   e   f   g.   h   i

(d) LUNEVILLE, France. Keller and Guerin, owners. Fayence. 1778. (e) VIENNA, Austria. Claudius Herr, painter. Late 18th-early 19th century. (f) KIEV, Russia. Porcelain. 1798-1850. (g) KIEV, Russia. Fayence. Painted. 1798-1850. (h) KIEL, Germany. Fayence. 1758. (i) KIEL, Germany. Tannich and Kleffel, owners. Fayence. Painted gold or color. 1763.

Kishere
Kishere   Mortlake   Klentsch   K.L.HMULLER
1875

j   k   l   m

(j-k) MORTLAKE, Great Britain. Joseph Kishere, potter. Stoneware. 1800-1811. (l) KLENTSCH, Germany. Porcelain. Circa 1835. (m) NEW YORK, New York, U.S.A. Union Porcelain Works. After 1876.

KLUM   KNAPPER AND BLACKHURST   **KODAU**   **KOSMO**   K.T.&K. CHINA

a   b   c   d   e

(a) KLUM, Germany. Porcelain. 1800-1850. (b) GREAT BRITAIN. Knapper and Blackhurst. Circa 1850. (c) CHODAU, Germany. Est. 1804. (d) EAST LIVERPOOL, Ohio, U.S.A. Smith-Phillips China Company. Late 19th century. (e) EAST LIVERPOOL, Ohio, U.S.A. Knowles, Taylor, and Knowles. Est. 1854.

f   g   h   i   j   k

SECTION L
See also Sections
I, J, Lines

(f) ARDUS, France. Fayence. 1739-1876. (g-h) PARIS, France. Jean-Joseph Lassia, proprietor. Porcelain. 1774-1784. (i) THURINGIA, Germany. Limbach, factory. Porcelain. 1772-1788. (j) PARIS, France. Jean-Joseph Lassia, proprietor. Porcelain. 1774-1784. (k) THURINGIA, Germany. Limbach, factory. Hard paste. 1772-1788.

l   m   n   o   p   q

(l) PARIS, France. Jean-Joseph Lassia, proprietor. Hard paste. 1774-1784. (m) THURINGIA, Germany. Limbach, factory. Hard paste. Painted red. 1772. (n) THURINGIA, Germany. Limbach, factory. Hard paste. 1772. (o) NORD, France. Valenciennes, factory. Fayence. 1735-1780. (p) TOURS, France. Fayence. Est. 1750. (q) BUEN RETIRO, Spain. Soft paste. 1759-1808.

a   b   c   d   e   f

(a) ARDUS, France. Fayence. 1739-1876. (b) HOLLAND. De
Metale Pot (The Metal Pot). Fayence. Delft. 1667. (c) OIRON,
France. Henri Deux ware (may have been made at Saint-Por-
chaire). 1676. (d) APREY, France. Fayence. Est. 1744. (e-f) THU-
RINGIA, Germany. Limbach, factory. Hard paste. 1772-1788.

g   h   i   j   k   l

(g-h) FRANCE. Louis Brancas, Comte de Lauraguais, invented
hard paste. Circa 1763. (i-j) LUXEMBOURG, Belgium. Circa 1770.
(k) SEPTFONTAINES, Germany. Villeroy and Boch, potters. 1766.
(l) THURINGIA, Germany Limbach, factory. Porcelain. 1772-1788.

m   n   o   p   q   r

(m) LUXEMBOURG, Belgium. Circa 1770. (n-o-p-q-r) THURIN-
GIA, Germany. Limbach, factory. Hard paste. 1772-1788.

a   b   c   d   e

(a) BRUSSELS, Belgium. L. Crette, porcelain-decorator. Hard paste. Painted. 1791-1803. (b) ROUEN, France. Hubert Lettellier, potter. Cream-colored ware. 1781. (c) SINCENY, France. Joseph Le Cerf, painter. 1773. (d) HOLLAND. Lucas van Kessel. Fayence. Delft. 1675. (e) THURINGIA, Germany. Limbach, factory. Hard paste. 1772.

f   g   h   i   j

(f) THURINGIA, Germany. Limbach, factory. Hard paste. 1772.
(g) THURINGIA, Germany. Bernburg, factory. Fayence. 1725.
(h) THURINGIA, Germany. Limbach, factory. Hard paste. Painted red, black, purple. 1772. (i) DRYVILLE, Pennsylvania, U.S.A. Lewis K. Tomlinson. Impressed. Circa 1875. (j) NORD, France. Valenciennes, factory. Fayence, hard paste. 1785.

L.L.   E$ $\overset{fM}{\underset{W}{\lambda}}$ Lo⋈   Lo   ''M·I6₂7

k   l   m   n   o

(k) LILLE, France. Hard paste. 1784. (l) HOLLAND. J. Mesch. Fayence. Delft. 1667. (m) WEESP, Holland. Porcelain. 1759. (n) ST. CLOUD, France. Fayence, porcelain. 1678-1766. (o) TUS-CANY, Italy. Montelupo, factory. Brown and black pottery. 17th century.

a   b   c   d   e

(a) LEEDS, Great Britain. Soft paste. Est. 1760. (b-c-d-e) MOUS-
TIERS, France. Clerissy's, factory. Joseph Olery, painter. Fayence.
1721-1749.

⟨PK   ℝ   𝔎   ℒS   L·S   ℒS

f   g   h   i   j   k

(f) HOLLAND. De Lampetkan (The Ewer). Widow of Gerardus
Brouwer, owner. Fayence. Delft. Painted blue. 1764. (g) BOR-
DEAUX, France. Lahrens and Rateau. Hard paste. Painted. 1828.
(h) REGENSBURG, Germany. Porcelain-decorating shop. Painted
blue. 1782. (i-j-k) SAINT YRIEIX, France. La Seynie, factory. Hard
paste. 1774.

l   m   n   o   p

(l-m) SCEAUX, France. Jacques Chapelle, proprietor. Soft paste.
1748-1794. (n) SAINT YRIEIX, France. La Seynie, factory. Hard
paste. 1774. (o) VINOVO, Italy. Porcelain. Underglaze blue or incised. 1776-1815. (p) HOLLAND. De Fortuyn (The Fortune). L. v.
Dale. Fayence. Delft. 1692.

a   b   c   d   e

(a-b) HOLLAND. De Klauw (The Claw). Fayence. Delft. 1662.
(c) TEINITZ, Bohemia. Count Wrtby, founder. Lead-glazed earthenware. 1801. (d) WHEELING, West Virginia, U.S.A. Wheeling Pottery Company. Est. 1879. (e) HANLEY, Great Britain. Lakin, potter. Late 18th and early 19th centuries.

LAKIN & POOLE   LAMPRECHT   *Langley Ware*

f   g   h

(f) HANLEY, Great Britain. Lakin and Poole, potters. Late 18th and early 19th centuries. (g) VIENNA, Austria. Georg Lamprecht, painter. 1772-1784. (h) NOTTINGHAM, Great Britain. Lovatt and Lovatt. Late 19th and early 20th centuries.

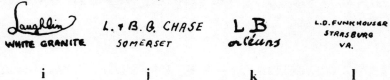

Laughlin WHITE GRANITE   L. & B. G. CHASE SOMERSET   LB *orléans*   L.D. FUNKHOUSER STRASBURG VA.

i   j   k   l

(i) EAST LIVERPOOL, Ohio, U.S.A. Homer Laughlin China Company. Printed. Est. 1872. (j) SOMERSET, Massachusetts, U.S.A. L. and B. G. Chase. Impressed. Circa 1850. (k) LOIRET, France. Orleans, factory. 1753-1812. (l) STRASBURG, Virginia, U.S.A. L. D. Funkhouser. Impressed. Circa 1900.

LEEDS POTTERY   LEEDS ✴ POTTERY

a   b   c

(a-b-c) LEEDS, Great Britain. Creamware. Est. 1760.

Le françois

Lefebvre a paris   à   LEHEW & CO.
                          Caen   STRASBURG, VA.

d   e   f

(d) PARIS, France. 1786. (e) CALVADOS, France. Caen, factory.
Hard paste. 1793. (f) STRASBURG, Virginia, U.S.A. Lehew and
Company. Impressed. Circa 1885.

                                              Lerosey
LEHMAN ⚜ RIEDINGER LELAND.   *Lunardus* // Rue de la paix

g   h   i   j

(g) POUGHKEEPSIE, New York, U.S.A. Louis, Lehman, and
Philip Riedinger (Rudinger). 1855. (h) EAST LIVERPOOL, Ohio,
U.S.A. C. C. Thompson Pottery Company. Est. 1888. (i) HOL-
LAND. L. v. Amsterdam. Fayence. Delft. 1721. (j) PARIS, France.
Lerosey, artist. Circa 1820.

a   b   c   d

(**a**) PARIS, France. Circa 1825. (**b**) HUNTINGTON, New York, U.S.A. Lewis and Gardiner (Gardner). Impressed. Circa 1840. (**c**) HUNTINGTON, New York, U.S.A. Lewis and Lewis. Impressed. Circa 1860. (**d**) UTICA, New York, U.S.A. L. F. Field. Circa 1865.

L.H. WORKS   *Liberty*   lille   LIPPERT & HAAS
IN
SCHLAGGENWALD   LISBOA

e   f   g   h   i

(**e**) NEWPORT, Ohio, U.S.A. Laban H. Works. Impressed. Circa 1845. (**f**) WELLSVILLE, Ohio, U.S.A. Pioneer Pottery Company. Circa 1890. (**g**) LILLE, France. Fayence. Painted. 1711. (**h**) SCHLAGGENWALD, Germany. Lippert and Haas, potters. 1832-1846. (**i**) LISBON, Portugal. Fayence. 1773.

L. NORTON & CO.
BENNINGTON
VT.   L. NORTON
BENNINGTON
VT.   L. NORTON & SON
BENNINGTON
VT.

j   k   l

(**j**) BENNINGTON, Vermont, U.S.A. Luman Norton. Impressed. Circa 1825. (**k**) BENNINGTON, Vermont, U.S.A. Luman Norton. Impressed. Circa 1830. (**l**) BENNINGTON, Vermont, U.S.A. Luman Norton and Son. Impressed. Circa 1835.

Longport   LONHUDA   Lósanti   LOUIS LEHMAN
            LE

a   b   c   d

(a) LONGPORT, Great Britain. Fayence. Printed red. 1793. (b)
STEUBENVILLE, Ohio, U.S.A. Lonhuda Pottery Compnay. Est.
1892. (c) CINCINNATI, Ohio, U.S.A. M. L. McLaughlin. Est. 1876.
(d) POUGHKEEPSIE, New York, U.S.A. Louis Lehman. Impressed. Circa 1852.

LOVATT LANGLEY MILL ENGLAND   OUWCLS WELLER   L P Kan   L. SOLON   L. W. FENTON St. Johnsbury Vt.

e   f   g   h   i

(e) ZANESVILLE, Ohio, U.S.A. S. A. Weller. Late 19th century.
(f) NOTTINGHAM, Great Britain. Lovatt and Lovatt. Late 19th-
early 20th century. (g) HOLLAND. De Lampetkan (The Ewer).
Widow of Gerardus Brouwer, owner. Fayence. Delft. Painted blue.
1764. (h) STOKE-ON-TRENT, Great Britain. Minton, factory. L.
M. Solon, artist. Circa 1900. (i) ST. JOHNSBURY, Vermont, U.S.A.
L. W. Fenton. Impressed. Circa 1840.

SECTION M   M   M   M   M   M   M
See also Sections
N, Lines   i   k   l   m   n   o

(j) MARIEBERG, Sweden. Fayence. 1758. (k) MARANS, France.
Pierre Roussencq, founder. Fayence. Est. 1740. (l) HANOVER,
Germany. Magdeburg, factory. Fayence. 18th century. (m) STOKE-
ON-TRENT, Great Britain. Minton, factory. Underglaze blue. 1820-
1830. (n) SINCENY, France. Fayence. Painted. 1864. (o) ROUEN,
France. Jacques Maugrard, potter. Fayence. 1722.

a   b   c   d   e   f

(a) MARANS, France. Pierre Roussencq, founder. Fayence. Est.
1740. (b) MATHAULT, France. Fayence. Second half 18th century.
(c) OUDE LOOSDRECHT, Holland. Johannes de Mol, owner.
Hard paste. Painted blue and impressed. 1771. (d) MARIEBERG,
Sweden. Fayence. 1758. (e) HOLLAND. De Vier Helden Van
Roome (The Four Roman Heroes). Fayence. Delft. 1713. (f) HOL-
LAND. De Vier Helden Van Roome (The Four Roman Heroes).
Fayence. Delft. 1713.

g   h   i   j   k

(g) ARNOLDI, Germany. Est. 1808. (h) MOUSTIERS, France.
Fayence. 18th century. (i) CINCINNATI, Ohio, U.S.A. M. L. Mc-
Laughlin. Est. 1876. (j) MENNECY, France. Porcelain. 1734-1773.
(k) HOLLAND. H. v. Middeldyk. Fayence. Delft. 1764.

l   m   n   o   p

(l) HOLLAND. T'Hart (The Stag). J. Mes. Fayence. Delft. 1661.
(m) HEREND, Hungary. Moritz Fischer, founder. Hard paste.
Painted blue. 1839. (n) MOUSTIERS, France. Joseph Olery,
founder. Fayence. Est. 1738. (o) CINCINNATI, Ohio, U.S.A. Rookwood Pottery Company. Impressed. Est. 1879. (p) MENNECY,
France. Soft paste porcelain. 1773.

a   b   c   d

(a) HOLLAND. T'Hart (The Stag). Fayence. Delft. 1764. (b-c)
OUDE LOOSDRECHT, Holland. Johannes de Mol, founder. Hard
paste. Underglaze blue or color. 1771-1784. (d) ETOILLES, France.
Monier and Pelleve, founders. Hard paste. Est. 1768.

MP   *MP*   MP   M.P   M.P.

e   f   g   h   i

(e) HOLLAND. De Metale Pot (The Metal Pot). Fayence. Delft.
Painted blue. 1639. (f) HOLLAND. De Metale Pot (The Metal
Pot). Fayence. Delft. 1639. (g) ROUEN, France. Pierre Mouchard,
potter. 1740. (h) OPORTO, Portugal. Rocha Soare. Fayence.
Painted gold. 1700. (i) MIRAGAYA, Portugal. Fayence. Last half
18th century.

MP.   M PM   M8.   MM   M·J·J.

j   k   l   m   n

(j) ETOILLES, France. Monier and Pelleve, founders. Hard paste.
Est. 1768. (k) DRESDEN, Germany. Meissner Porzellan Manufak-
tur. Hard paste. 1723. (l) SHELTON, Great Britain. Fayence.
Printed. 1685. (m) PARIS, France. Pont-aux-Chaoux. 1784. (n)
AMUND, Germany. Fayence. 1750.

a   b   c   d   e

(a) ROUEN, France. Michel-Mathieu and Michel Vallet, potters.
1757. (b) HOLLAND. De Twee Wildemans (The Two Savages).
M. v. d. Bogarert. Fayence. Delft. 1750. (c) HOLLAND. Fayence.
Delft. Painted blue. 1700. (d) ROUEN, France. Maugrard, potter.
Fayence. 1722. (e) GERMANY. Schmidt Brothers. Est. 1847.

f   g   h

(f) BURSLEM, Great Britain. Staffordshire. 1830. (g) GREAT
BRITAIN. MacIntyre. Circa 1860. (h) EAST LIVERPOOL, Ohio,
U.S.A. Globe Pottery Company. Circa 1890.

i   j   k

(i) PERTH AMBOY, New Jersey, U.S.A. Henry Stockwell, artist.
1830. (j) CHEESEQUAKE, New Jersey, U.S.A. Joshua Letts. Circa
1810. (k) SAYREVILLE, New Jersey, U.S.A. Xerxes Price. Impressed. Circa 1800.

MAINE. **MANN & CO.**   **MANTELL + THOMAS**   *Manufactured by Jos Hemphill Philad.*
              HANLEY   **PENN YAN**

a   b   c   d

(a) EAST LIVERPOOL, Ohio, U.S.A. Knowles, Taylor and
Knowles, Est. 1854. (b) HANLEY, Great Britain. Mann and Com-
pany. 19th century. (c) YATES COUNTY, New York, U.S.A. Pen
Yan Pottery. Circa 1840. (d) PHILADELPHIA, Pennsylvania,
U.S.A. Joseph Hemphill. Circa 1835.

MARAN

Manifre de   **1754**
M.M·.   MARKELL, IMMON & CO.
Guerhard et   MANUFACTURED BY   AKRON
Lihl à Paris. OTT&BREWER   **MAP** **R**   O.
                TRENTON N J USA

e   f   g   h   i

(e) PARIS, France. Guerhard, potter. Hard paste. 1786-1829.
(f) TRENTON, New Jersey, U.S.A. Ott and Brewer. Circa 1875.
(g) PARIS, France. Morelle, potter. Hard paste. Painted blue. 1725.
(h) MARANS, France. Pierre Roussencq, founder. Fayence. 1740.
(i) AKRON, Ohio, U.S.A. Markell, Immon, and Company. Impressed. Circa 1870.

MARTIN CRAFTS   **MASON & RUSSELL**
NASHUA, N.H.   **CORTLAND**
                       N.Y.   **MASON'S CAMBRIAN**
                                           ARGIL

j   k   l

(j) NASHUA, New Hampshire, U.S.A. Martin Crafts. Impressed.
Circa 1850. (k) CORTLAND, New York, U.S.A. Mason and Russell. Impressed. Circa 1870. (l) FENTON, Great Britain. Mason.
1813.

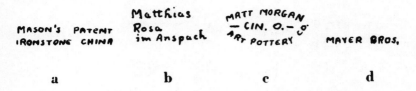

Matthias
Rosa
im Anspach

MASON's PATENT
IRONSTONE CHINA

MATT MORGAN
— CIN. O. — o
ART POTTERY

MAYER BROS.

a   b   c   d

(a) FENTON, Great Britain. Fayence. Printed. 1813. (b) ANS-BACH, Germany. Fayence. 1730. (c) CINCINNATI, Ohio, U.S.A. Matt Morgan Art Pottery Company. Circa 1885. (d) HANLEY, Great Britain. Circa 1820.

May' & Newb'   M&B
FELSPAR PORCELAIN   Mo B
orleâun

e   f   g

(e) LANE END, Great Britain. Fayence. Impressed or printed. 1800. (f) STOKE-ON-TRENT, Great Britain. Minton and Boyle. Impressed. 1836-1841. (g) ORLEANS, France. Hard paste. Circa 1760.

M Borelli

Mc CARTHY BROS.
SOMERVILLE
MASS.

M
CHINA
L

m
Clermont ferrand
D'auvergne
21 jauier 1736

h   i   j   k

(h) SAVONA, Italy. M. Forelli. 1740. (i) SOMERVILLE, Massachusetts, U.S.A. Circa 1870. (j) TRENTON, New Jersey, U.S.A. Maddock Pottery Company. Circa 1900. (k) CLERMONT-FERRAND, France. Fayence. 1730.

MELROSE

M.C. WEBSTER   Meigh   MELLORIA   T.   M·C·A 1750. J.A
HARTFORD

a   b   c   d   e

(a) HARTFORD, Connecticut, U.S.A. M. C. Webster and Son. Impressed. Circa 1850. (b) HANLEY, Great Britain. Pottery. Impressed. 1780. (c) TRENTON, New Jersey, U.S.A. Crescent Pottery Company. Est. 1881. (d) EAST LIVERPOOL, Ohio, U.S.A. C. C. Thompson Pottery Company. Circa 1880. (e) MOUSTIERS, France. Hard paste, soft paste. 18th century.

MIDDLES BRO
POTTERY CO.

f   g   h   i

(f) MIDDLESBOROUGH, Great Britain. Earthenware. Impressed. 1845. (g) MILAN, Italy. Fayence. 18th century. (h) MILAN, Italy. Felice Clerici, potter. 1745. (i) LIMOGES, France. After 1891.

M.Imp^{le}
de Sevres   MINER   MINTON.   MINTON. & BOYLE

j.   k   l   m

(j) SEVRES, France. Hard paste, soft paste. Painted red. 1804-1809. (k) SYMMES CREEK, Ohio, U.S.A. William Miner. Impressed. Circa 1870. (l) STOKE-ON-TRENT, Great Britain. Minton. 1868. (m) STOKE-ON-TRENT, Great Britain. Minton and Boyle. 1836-1845.

MINTON & CO.   MIRAGAÏA   MN^{u} Sèvres   M. MASON

a   b   c   d

(a) STOKE-ON-TRENT, Great Britain. Minton. Circa 1870. (b)
MIRAGAYA, Portugal. Fayence. 18th century. (c) SEVRES, France.
Soft paste. Stenciled red. 1803. (d) FENTON, Great Britain. Late
18th century.

M. & N.   Moitte.   MOORE & CO. SOUTHWICK   MORAVIAN

e   f   g   h

(e) HANLEY, Great Britain. Mayer and Newbold, potters. First
half 19th century. (f) PARIS, France. Clignancourt, factory. Est.
1771. (g) SOUTHWICK, Great Britain. Pottery and hard paste.
1803. (h) DOYLESTOWN, Pennsylvania, U.S.A. Henry C. Mercer.
Circa 1890.

Morley & Ashworth HANLEY   MORTLOCK   MOX   M: J^{ns}Cookworthy's Factory Plymouth 1770   M. Sansont

i   j   k   l   m

(i) SHELTON, Great Britain. Staffordshire. Circa 1850. (j) SWIN-
TON, Great Britain. Rockingham Pottery Works. William Brameld,
owner. 1745-1842. (k) ALCORA, Spain. Est. 1750. (l) PLYM-
OUTH, Great Britain. Hard paste. Painted blue. 1770. (m) VAL-
SOUS MEUDON, France. White earthenware. 1802-1818.

M Trecchi   M.WOODRUFF CORTLAND N.Y   MYATT WHIELDON   MYERS & HALL MOGADORE

a   b   c   d

(a) MILAN, Italy. Fayence. 18th century. (b) CORTLAND, New York, U.S.A. Madison Woodruff. Impressed. Circa 1870. (c) FENTON, Great Britain. Thomas Whieldon. Impressed. Circa 1775. (d) MOGADORE, Ohio, U.S.A. Myers and Hall. Impressed. Circa 1875.

SECTION N
See also Sections
M, Lines

e   f   g   h   i

(e) NIDERVILLER, France. Fayence. Est. 1754. (f) SHELTON, Great Britain. New Hall, factory. Painted red. Est. 1777. (g) DERBY, Great Britain. Incised blue, red. Circa 1770. (h) NIDERVILLER, France. Count Custine period. Fayence, porcelain. 1770-1793. (i) OLEAN, New York, U.S.A. I. H. Wands. Impressed. Circa 1860.

j   k   l   m   n

(j) NEVERS, France. Fayence. Circa 1700. (k) NEVERS, France. Fayence. Circa 1700. (l) NIDERVILLER, France. Hard paste. 1780-1800. (m) LIMBACH, Germany. Porcelain. Est. 1772. (n) BRISTOL, Great Britain. Pottery, porcelain. Overglaze blue, gold. 18th century.

$\mathcal{N}$+5 $\overset{10}{\mathsf{N}}$ N H N.H N1β

a   b   c   d   e

(a) THE HAGUE, Holland. Porcelain. Painted red. Est. 1773.
(b) PINXTON, Great Britain. Soft paste. Red. Circa 1800. (c)
NIDERVILLER, France. Count Custine period. Fayence, porcelain.
1770-1793. (d) WROTHAM, Great Britain. 17th century. (e)
ROUEN, France. Jean-Nicolas Bellanger, potter. Fayence. 1788.

$\mathcal{N}.\mathcal{D}.$ N.G.   N.G.F   N.J.H $\mathcal{N}$

f   g   h   i   j

(f) BUEN RETIRO, Spain. Soft paste. 1759-1808. (g-h) GIESS-
HUBEL, Germany. Porcelain and earthenware. 1803-1850. (i) CIN-
CINNATI, Ohio, U.S.A. Matt Morgan Art Pottery Company. Est.
1883. (j) SHELTON, Great Britain. Painted black. Est. 1777.

k   l   m   n

(k) URBINO, Italy. Pottery. 16th century. (l) THURINGIA, Germany. Ilmenau, factory. Christian Nonne and Roesch, owners. Porcelain. 1786. (m) NANTGARW, Wales. Hard paste. Impressed. 1813.
(n) NANTGARW, Wales. Hard paste. Painted red. 1811.

N...
a
Paris   Nassau?   Nast   NATHAN CLARK

a   b   c   d

(a) PARIS, France. Jean-Nepomucene-Herman Nast, porcelain manufacturer. Painted red. 1754-1817. (b) TRENTON, New Jersey, U.S.A. Mercer Pottery Company. Circa 1869. (c) PARIS, France. Jean-Nepomucene-Herman Nast, porcelain manufacturer. Hard paste. Stenciled red. 1754-1817. (d) ATHENS, New York, U.S.A. Nathan Clark. Circa 1830.

NATHAN CLARK LYONS   Neale   Neale & Co.   Neale & Palmer

e   f   g   h

(e) ATHENS, New York, U.S.A. Nathan Clark. Circa 1830. (f) HANLEY, Great Britain. Fayence. Impressed. 1776. (g) HANLEY, Great Britain. Neale and Company. Staffordshire. 1778. (h) HANLEY, Great Britain. Neale and Palmer. Staffordshire. 1786.

Neale & Wilton   Nasid   Neeld   Neumark

i   j   k   l

(i) HANLEY, Great Britain. Staffordshire. Circa 1780. (j-k) HANLEY, Great Britain. Pottery. Impressed. 1780. (l) NEUMARK, Germany. Porcelain. Impressed. 1832.

NEWCASTLE   NEWCOMB COLLEGE   New Hall   N. FURMAN NO.39 PECK SLIP, N.Y.   N & H PRAG

a   b   c   d   e

(a) NEWCASTLE-ON-TYNE, Great Britain. Pottery. Impressed. 1800. (b) NEW ORLEANS, Louisiana, U.S.A. Est. 1896. (c) SHELTON, Great Britain. New Hall factory. Painted red. Est. 1777. (d) CHEESEQUAKE, New Jersey, U.S.A. Noah Furman. Circa 1850. (e) PRAGUE, Bohemia. Lead-glazed earthenware. 1810-1862.

NICHOLS & ALFORD MANUFACTURERS BURLINGTON, VT.   NICHOLS + BOYNTON BURLINGTON, VT.   Nider·

f   g   h

(f) BURLINGTON, Vermont, U.S.A. Nichols and Alford. Circa 1855. (g) BURLINGTON, Vermont, U.S.A. Nichols and Boynton. Impressed. Circa 1855. (h) NIDERVILLER, France. Fayence. Est. 1754.

NORTON & FENTON BENNINGTON, VT.   NORWICH   NOTTN. 1703

i   j   k

(i) BENNINGTON, Vermont, U.S.A. Norton and Fenton. Stoneware. Impressed. Circa 1845. (j) NORWICH, Connecticut, U.S.A. Charles Lathrop. Impressed. Circa 1790. (k) NOTTINGHAM, Great Britain. Pottery. 1703.

a   b   c

(a-b) BASSANO, Italy. Soft paste. Circa 1760. (c) ALT-ROHLAU,
Bohemia. August Nowotny, owner. Pottery, porcelain. 1813.

SECTION O O O oB oP OS
See also Sections
Circle and Sign,
Crown and Circle,   d   e   f   g   h
Star and Sun

(d) BOW, Great Britain. Porcelain. Circa 1750. (e) ST. PETERS-
BURG, Russia. Porcelain. Circa 1762. (f) MENNECY-VILLEROY,
France. Porcelain, fayence. Est. 1734. (g) MENNECY-VILLEROY,
France. Porcelain, fayence. Painted blue. Circa 1773. (h) ANS-
BACH, Bavaria. George Oswald, painter, potter. 1692-1733.

O.V.   ·OY·   O.&B.   O.B.
                         CHINA   OLDFIELD & CO.

i   j   k   l   m

(i) WHEELING, West Virginia, U.S.A. Ohio Valley China Company. Circa 1890. (j) MOUSTIERS, France. Olerys and Laugier,
managers. Hard paste, soft paste. 1739. (k-l) TRENTON, New
Jersey, U.S.A. Ott and Brewer. Circa 1880. (m) BRAMPTON, Great
Britain. Brownware. Circa 1825.

OLIVER   Opaque China
A PARIS Opaque China B.B.&I. Opaque China
             B and C

a   b   c   d

(a) PARIS, France. Olivier, potter. Fayence. Late 18th century.
(b) CAMBRIAN, Wales. Earthenware. Circa 1807. (c) SWANSEA,
Great Britain. Baker, Bevans, and Irwin. Circa 1830. (d) GREAT
BRITAIN. Bridgwood and Clark. 1857.

OPAQUE CHINA OPAQUE O. P. Co. O.P.Co. O.P. CO.
SWANSEA PORCELAIN CHINA. IMPERIAL SYRACUSE
               CHINA

e   f   g   h   i

(e) SWANSEA, Wales. Circa 1840. (f) GREAT BRITAIN. Old
Hall Works, factory. Earthenware. Circa 1800. (g-h-i) SYRACUSE,
New York, U.S.A. Onondaga Pottery Company. Est. 1871.

ORCUT, BELDING & CO. ORCUTT, GUILFORD & Co. ORCUTT HUMISTON & CO.
ASHFIELD,   ASHFIELD, MASS.   TROY, N.Y.
MASS

j   k   l

(j-k) ASHFIELD, Massachusetts, U.S.A. Orcutt, Belding and Company. Impressed. 1850. (l) TROY, New York. U.S.A. Orcutt, Humiston and Company. Impressed. Circa 1855.

a   b   c   d

(a) COBRIDGE, Great Britain. J. and G. Alcock. Est. 1843. (b) LOIRET, France. Duke of Orleans, patron. Est. 1753. (c-d) ZANESVILLE, Ohio, U.S.A. J. B. Owens Pottery Company. Circa 1890.

SECTION P
See also Sections
B, Lines

e   f   g   h   i   j

(e-f) LIVERPOOL, Great Britain. James and John Pennington, potters and painters. Middle 18th century. (g-h) LIVERPOOL, Great Britain. James and John Pennington, potters and painters. Pottery and hard paste. Painted gold or color. 1760. (i-j) DERBYSHIRE, Great Britain. Pinxton, factory. Soft paste. Painted. 1796-1801.

P P' P'' P P P

k   l   m   n   o   p

(k-l) SILESIA, Germany. Count Leopold von Proskau, factory owner. Fayence. 1763-1769. (m) NYMPHENBERG, Germany. Porcelain. Impressed or incised. Est. 1755. (n) PRAGUE, Germany. Lead-glazed earthenware. 1810-1862. (o) PHILADELPHIA, Pennsylvania, U.S.A. Bonnin and Morris. Incised. Circa 1770. (p) LIVERPOOL, Great Britain. Seth Pennington, potter. Painted gold or color. Second half 18th century.

a   b   c   d   e   f

(a) LIVERPOOL, Great Britain. Seth Pennington, potter. Painted gold and colors. Second half 18th century. (b) HOLLAND. De Porceleyne Schootel (The Porcelain Dish). Johannes Pennis, potter. Fayence. Delft. 1723-1763. (c) KIEL, Germany. J. S. Tannich, founder. Fayence. 1763. (d) DERBYSHIRE, Great Britain. Pinxton factory. Soft paste. 1796-1813. (e) PRAGUE, Germany. Lead-glazed earthenware. 1795-1810. (f) DERBYSHIRE, Great Britain. Pinxton factory. Soft paste. 1796-1813 (mark doubtful).

g   h   i   j   k   l

(g-h-i) HOLLAND. De Porceleyne Schootel (The Porcelain Dish). Johannes Pennis, potter. Fayence. Delft. 1723-1763. (j) APREY, France. Fayence. Est. 1744. (k) SAINT CLOUD, France. Fayence, porcelain. Est. 1758. (l) HOLLAND. De Metale Pot (The Metal Pot). Fayence. Delft. Circa 1639.

m   n   o   p   q   r

(m) HOLLAND. Jacob Pietersz, potter. Fayence. Delft. 1663-1682. (n) HOLLAND. De Porceleyne Schootel (The Porcelain Dish). Fayence. Delft. 1759. (o) LILLE, France. Phillippe-Auguste Petit, potter. Painted color. 1778. (p) HOLLAND. De Porceleyne Byl (The Porcelain Hatchet). Fayence. Delft. 1679. (q) CHANTILLY, France. Pigory, owner. Soft paste. Early 19th century. (r) CINCINNATI, Ohio, U.S.A. Rookwood Pottery Company. 1886.

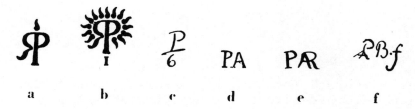

a   b   c   d   e   f

(a-b) CINCINNATI, Ohio, U.S.A. Rookwood Pottery Company.
One flame added to mark for each year after 1886. (c) SILESIA,
Germany. Count Leopold von Proskau, founder. Fayence. 1783-1793.
(d) ROUEN, France. Fayence. Painted color. 16th century. (e)
ROUEN, France. Fayence. 1720. (f) MOUSTIERS, France. Fay-
ence. Est. 1738.

$$\mathcal{\widehat{A}J} \quad \textbf{PB} \quad \textit{V} \quad PBC \quad \textit{P·c} \quad \textbf{P·C}$$

g   h   i   j   k   l

(g) MOUSTIERS, France. Fayence. Est. 1738. (h) PARIS, France.
Circa 1800. (i) HOLLAND. De Fortuyn (The Fortune). Fayence.
Delft. Painted blue. 1691. (j) GARD, France. Nimes, factory. Pottery. Impressed. 1830. (k) ALCORA, Spain. Fayence, porcelain. Est.
1727. (l) NEVERS, France. Fayence. 16th century.

m   n   o   p   q   r

(m) ROUEN, France. Paul Caussy, potter. Fayence. From 1707.
(n) HOLLAND. Jacobus and Asriaen Pynaker, Albrecht de Keyser,
potters. Fayence. Delft. Painted blue. 1680. (o) HOLLAND. De
Porceleyne Fles (The Porcelain Bottle). Pieter van Doorne, potter.
Fayence. Delft. Painted blue. 1764. (p) ROUEN, France. Pierre
Dumont, painter. Second half 18th century. (q) MOUSTIERS,
France. Hard paste, soft paste. Est. 1738. (r) STRASBURG, France.
Paul Hannong, proprietor. Underglaze blue. 1740-1760.

a   b   c   d   e   f

(a) STRASBURG, France. Paul Hannong, proprietor. Underglaze blue. 1740-1760. (b) FRANKENTHAL, Germany. Paul Hannong, director. Porcelain. Circa 1755. (c-d-e) STRASBURG, France. Paul Hannong, proprietor. Porcelain. Underglaze blue. 1740-1760. (f) HOLLAND. Philip Wouvermans, artist. Fayence. Delft. Painted. Circa 1600.

g   h   i   j   k   l

(g) ROUEN, France. Circa 1720. (h) HOLLAND. De Drie Porceleyne Fleschen (The Three Porcelain Bottles). Fayence. Delft. 1672. (i) HOLLAND. De Drie Vergulde Astonne (The Three Golden Ash Barrels). Gerrit Pietersz Kam, potter. Fayence. Delft. 1674-1700. (j) HOLLAND. De Drie Porceleyne Fleschen (The Three Porcelain Bottles). Fayence. Delft. 1672. (k-l) PARIS, France. 1786-1793.

m   n   o   p   q   r

(m) PARIS, France. 1786-1793. (n-o) DERBYSHIRE, Great Britain. Pinxton factory. Soft paste. Est. 1796. (p) ROUEN, France. Pierre Dumont, potter. After 1750. (q) HOLLAND. De Romeyn (The Roman). Petrus van Meerum, potter. Fayence. Delft. Painted blue. 1764. (r) DERBYSHIRE, Great Britain. Pinxton, factory. Soft paste. Est. 1796.

a   b   c   d   e

(a) ROUEN, France. Fayence. Circa 1720. (b) NEVERS, France. Fayence. 1630. (c) CHODAU, Germany. Circa 1805. (d) HOLLAND. De Porceleyne Fles (The Porcelain Bottle). Pieter van Doorne, artist. Fayence. Delft. Painted blue. 1764. (e) HOLLAND. De Fortuyn (The Fortune). P. van der Briel. Fayence. Delft. Painted blue. 1753-1769.

f   g   h   i

(f) HOLLAND. Fayence. Delft. 1725. (g-h) HOLLAND. De Romeyn (The Roman). Petrus van Meerum, potter. Fayence. Delft. Painted blue. 1764. (i) BURTON-ON-TRENT, Great Britain. Ashby Potter's Guild. Pottery. Est. 1909.

Paauwe   **PALME**   *Palme*   PAUL CUSHMAN

j   k   l   m

(j) HOLLAND. De Paauw (The Peacock). Fayence. Delft. 1729-1740. (k-l) SCHELTEN, Bohemia. S. L. Palme, artist. Porcelain. Impressed. Est. Circa 1840. (m) ALBANY, New York, U.S.A. Paul Cushman. Impressed. Circa 1815.

PAUL· CUSHMAN· STOE· WARE
FACTORY· 1809· HALF· A· MILE
WEST OF ALBANY GOAL *pa͠un* **P & B** *P. BELL*

a b c d

(a) ALBANY, New York, U.S.A. Paul Cushman. Impressed. Circa 1815. (b) HOLLAND. De Paauw (The Peacock). Fayence. Delft. 1729-1740. (c) HANLEY, Great Britain. Powell and Bishop. Impressed. Circa 1875. (d) WINCHESTER, Virginia, U.S.A. Peter Bell. Circa 1800.

P. CROSS
HARTFORD **PEACoCK POTTERY** **PEARL WARE** *Pennington*

e f g h

(e) HARTFORD, Connecticut, U.S.A. Peter Cross. Circa 1810. (f) FENTON, Great Britain. Foley China Works. 20th century. (g) LANE END, Great Britain. Chetham and Wooley, factory. Staffordshire. 18th and 19th centuries. (h) LIVERPOOL, Great Britain. Seth Pennington, potter. Hard paste, fayence. Impressed. Painted gold. 1760.

PEN YAN PEORIA ILLINOIS PETER KELLEY **PFALTZGRAFF POTTERY**

i j k l

(i) YATES COUNTY, New York, U.S.A. Pen Yan Pottery. Circa 1840. (j) PEORIA, Illinois, U.S.A. Peoria Pottery Company. Circa 1880. (k) PHILADELPHIA, Pennsylvania, U.S.A. Peter Kelley. Impressed. Circa 1840. (l) YORK, Pennsylvania, U.S.A. Pfaltzgraff Pottery. Impressed. Circa 1875.

Phillip Kline   *Phillips*   PHILLIPS & Co.

a   b   c

(a) CARVERSVILLE, Pennsylvania, U.S.A. Phillip Kline. Circa 1808. (b) LONGPORT, Great Britain. G. Phillips, potter. Blue-printed earthenware. 19th century. (c) SUNDERLAND, Great Britain. John Phillips, potter. Pottery. Printed color. 18th-19th century.

Phillips & C°
Sunderland. 1813   *"Phillips Longport"*   Phoenix Pottery

d   e   f

(d) SUNDERLAND, Great Britain. Pottery. 18th-19th century. (e) LONGPORT, Great Britain. G. Phillips, potter. Blue-printed earthenware. 19th century. (f) PHOENIXVILLE, Pennsylvania, U.S.A. Phoenix Pottery. Est. 1867.

Porcelaine Mousseline

Pinxton.   POINTONS   Limoges FRANCE   FRENCH T.P.W.

g   h   i   j

(g) DERBYSHIRE, Great Britain. Pinxton factory. Soft paste. 1796. (h) STOKE-ON-TRENT, Great Britain. Pointons. Late 19th century. (i) HAVILAND, France. Porcelain. Printed red, green. 1895. (j) TRENTON, New Jersey, U.S.A. Trenton Pottery Works. Late 19th century.

a   b   c

(**a**) MOULINS, France. Fayence. 1730. (**b**) PARIS, France. Hard paste. Painted red. 1773. (**c**) PLYMOUTH, Great Britain. Plymouth Pottery Company. 1850.

d   e   f   g

(**d**) BARBADOES NECK, New Jersey, U.S.A. P. P. Sanford. 18th century. (**e**) PRAGUE, Bohemia. Prager. Porcelain. 1810-1862. (**f**) FENTON, Great Britain. Felix Pratt, potter. Staffordshire. 1780-1820. (**g**) EAST LIVERPOOL, Ohio, U.S.A. Homer Laughlin China Company. Printed. Est. 1874.

h   i   j   k

(**h**) PUTNAM, Ohio, U.S.A. Prosper Rice. Impressed. Circa 1840. (**i**) SILESIA, Germany. Proskau, factory. Impressed. Est. 1763. (**j**) PARIS, France. Fayence. 1855. (**k**) HOLLAND. Piet Vizeer, painter. Fayence. Delft. 1752.

a   b   c   d   e   f

(a) THURINGIA, Germany. Rudolstadt, factory. Fayence. Est.
1720. (b) CHELSEA, Great Britain. Louis-Francois Roubiliac,
sculptor. Impressed. Circa 1738. (c) MARSEILLES, France. Porcelain. Est. 1766. (d) REGENSBURG, Germany. Porcelain decorating
shop. Painted blue. 1782. (e) THURINGIA, Germany. Gotha, factory. Hard paste. Est. 1757. (f) MARSEILLES, France. Joseph
Gaspard Robert, potter. Porcelain. Circa 1754.

g   h   i   j   k   l

(g) THURINGIA, Germany. Gotha, factory. Hard paste. Est. 1757.
(h) RUCKINGEN, Germany. Fayence. Est. 1720. (i) BRISTOL,
Great Britain. Porcelain. Circa 1750. (j) THURINGIA, Germany.
Gotha, factory. Hard paste. Est. 1757. (k) RATO, Portugal. Fayence. Painted yellow, violet. 1767. (l) BOW, Great Britain. Porcelain. 1750-1760.

m   n   o   p   q   r

(m) RENAC, France. Est. 1762. (n) ROUEN, France. 16th century. (o-p) THURINGIA, Germany. Rauenstein, factory. Porcelain.
1783. (q) MARSEILLES, France. Joseph Gaspard Robert, potter.
Porcelain. Circa 1754. (r) HOLLAND. De Roos (The Rose).
Fayence. Delft. Est. 1675.

a   b   c   d   e

(a) HOLLAND. De Roos (The Rose). Fayence. Delft. Est. 1675.
(b) MILAN, Italy. Fayence, porcelain. 1850. (c) HOLLAND. De
Boot (The Boat). Fayence. Delft. Est. 1667. (d) BOW, Great Britain. Porcelain. 1750-1760. (e) FAENZA, Italy. Fayence. Circa 1775.

f   g   h   i   j

(f) MARSEILLES, France. Joseph Gaspard Robert, potter. Fayence, porcelain. 1754-1793. (g) PARIS, France. Christopher Potter,
owner. Hard paste. 1789-1807. (h) PHILADELPHIA, Pennsylvania,
U.S.A. Richard Remmey. Impressed. Est. 1859. (i-j) SEVRES,
France. Hard paste, soft paste. Painted blue, gold. 1793-1804.

k   l   m   n   o

(k-l-m-n) SEVRES, France. Soft paste, hard paste. Painted blue,
gold. 1793-1804. (o) MARSEILLES, France. Joseph Gaspard Robert, potter. Fayence, porcelain. 1754-1793.

a   b   c   d   e

(a-b-c) REGENSBURG, Germany. Porcelain-decorating shop. 1793; or THURINGIA, Germany. Gotha, factory. William Rotberg, founder. Hard paste. Underglaze blue or impressed. These three marks are attributed to both factories. (d) MEISSEN, Germany. Hard paste. Underglaze blue. Circa 1730. (e) THURINGIA, Germany. Bernburg, factory. Fayence. Est. 1725.

R—n   RPM   RVK   ·R·X· $\mathcal{R}$ №¼ 𝓗

f   g   h   i   j

(f) THURINGIA, Germany. Rauenstein, factory. Hard paste. 1783. (g) HEGEWALD, Bohemia. Porcelain. 1850. (h) COLOGNE, Germany. Stoneware. Painted blue. 1600. (i) MARSEILLES, France. Joseph Gaspard Robert, potter. Fayence, porcelain. 1754-1793. (j) RORSTRAND, Sweden. Fayence. Circa 1760.

RAINFORTH & CO.   *Raleigh*   RALPH B. BEECH Patented Jan. 3, 1851 KENSINGTON, PA

k   l   m

(k) LEEDS, Great Britain. Rainforth, potter. Late 18th-early 19th century. (l) EAST LIVERPOOL, Ohio, U.S.A. United States Pottery Company. Est. 1846. (m) PHILADELPHIA, Pennsylvania, U.S.A. Ralph Beech. Impressed. Est. 1845.

RALPH SIMPSON   R·A·L·P·H·: T·A·Y·L·O·R

a   b

(a) GREAT BRITAIN. Ralph Simpson, potter. Slipware. 1707.
(b) GREAT BRITAIN. Ralph Taylor, potter. Slipware. 1697.

RALPH TOFT   RALPH • TURNOR   Ra Wood
                                  BURSLEM   R.B. & S.

c   d   e   f

(c) WROTHAM, Great Britain. Ralph Toft, potter. Slipware. 1677.
(d) GREAT BRITAIN. Ralph Turner, potter. Slipware. 1681.
(e) BURSLEM, Great Britain. Ralph Wood, potter. Salt-glazed
stoneware. 1749-1770. (f) LEEDS, Great Britain. Circa 1875.

R. COCHRAN & CO.   R G Remmey
   GLASGOW   R. DANIEL   R. Drach

g   h   i   j

(g) GLASGOW, Scotland. R. Cochran and Company. Circa 1860.
(h) PHILADELPHIA, Pennsylvania, U.S.A. Richard Remmey. Impressed. Est. 1859. (i) COBRIDGE, Great Britain. Ralph Daniel,
potter. 1750. (j) BEDMINSTER, Pennsylvania, U.S.A. Rudolf
Drach. Circa 1790.

Real
IRONSTONE   REED.   REGINA   REGINA   Reid & Co.
CHINA   C P. CO   H. & G.

a   b   c   d   e

(a) SHELTON, Great Britain. Job Ridgway, potter. Stone-china,
porcelain. 1802. (b) MEXBOROUGH, Great Britain. John Reed,
potter. Late 18th century. (c) EVANSVILLE, Indiana, U.S.A.
Crown Pottery Company. Est. 1891. (d) LONGTON, Great Britain.
Holland and Green. From 1850. (e) LIVERPOOL, Great Britain.
William Reid, potter. Porcelain. Impressed. 1755-1759.

Reinir   RENA   Rendsburg   RFB PORCELHNA
                         Duve   E SMC

f   g   h   i

(f) HOLLAND. De Romeyn (The Roman). Fayence. Delft. 1697.
(g) EVANSVILLE, Indiana, U.S.A. Crown Pottery Company. Est.
1891. (h) RENDSBURG, Germany. Fayence, lead-glazed earthenware. 1764-1818. (i) BUEN RETIRO, Spain. Soft paste. 1759-1808.

R Hancock fecit   RICHARD MARE   RICHEY & HAMILTON
                                 PALATINE, W. VA.

j   k   l

(j) WORCESTER, Great Britain. Hard paste. 1756-1774. (k)
GREAT BRITAIN. Richard Mare, potter. Slipware. 1697. (l) PAL-
ATINE, West Virginia, U.S.A. Richey and Hamilton. Blue. Circa
1875.

RIDGWAYS   RIDGWAY & SONS   *RIEDINGER + CARIE*
POUGHKEEPSIE   **RILEY**

a   b   c   d

(a-b) SHELTON, Great Britain. Job Ridgway, potter. 1794-1802.
(c) POUGHKEEPSIE, New York, U.S.A. Riedinger and Caire (Rudinger). Impressed. Circa 1875. (d) BURSLEM, Great Britain. J. and R. Riley, potters. Earthenware. Early 19th century.

R. & J.
Baddeley   R. M. W. & Co.   Robertson & Sons
CHELSEA KERAMIC
ART WORKS
C.K.A.W.   **ROCKET**

e   f   g   h

(e) SHELTON, Great Britain. Ralph and John Baddeley, proprietors. Salt-glazed stoneware. Impressed. 1750. (f) SHELTON, Great Britain. William Ridgway, Morley, Wear, potters. Staffordshire. Circa 1840. (g) CHELSEA, Massachusetts, U.S.A. James Robertson and Son. Impressed. Circa 1880. (h) EAST LIVERPOOL, Ohio, U.S.A. William Brunt Pottery Company. 1850-1895.

Rockingham
ROCKINGHAM   **ROGERS
JOHN**   **ROOKWOOD
1882**

i   j   k   l

(i-j) SWINTON, Great Britain. Rockingham, factory. Bramels and Company. Late 18th-early 19th century. (k) NEW YORK, New York, U.S.A. John Rogers. Terracotta. Circa 1875. (l) CINCINNATI, Ohio, U.S.A. Rookwood, factory. Impressed. 1882.

$\mathcal{R}_{00}\mathcal{K}^{w000}_{POTT^{\varepsilon R\gamma}_{CY.0.}}$ $\mathcal{R}_{00\mathcal{J}}$ $\mathcal{R}_{0}\mathcal{M}\frac{6}{3}$ $\mathcal{R}\dot{o}n\mathcal{H}\frac{10}{7}7^{0}$
$_{1881}$ $24\beta KY$
                                                                                 $\frac{C\mathcal{E}}{3}$

   a   b   c   d

(a) CINCINNATI, Ohio, U.S.A. Rookwood Pottery Company. Impressed. 1881. (b) HOLLAND. De Roos (The Rose). A. Cosijn, artist. Fayence. Delft. 1675. (c-d) RORSTRAND, Sweden. Fayence. Est. 1725.

$\mathcal{R}\ddot{o}n\mathcal{H}\frac{27}{8}67$ RORSTRAND   Rossi $\mathcal{R}ouy.$ $^{Royal\,B:}_{rcelan}$
CB 1785

   e.   f   g   h   i

(e) RORSTRAND, Sweden. Fayence. Est. 1725. (f) RORSTRAND, Sweden. Fayence, cream-colored ware. Est. 1725. (g) COIMBRA, Portugal. Fayence. 18th-early 19th century. (h) ROUY, France. Fayence. Est. 1790. (i) TRENTON, New Jersey, U.S.A. Burgess and Campbell. Est. 1879.

$^{SEMI\,PO}_{\mathcal{L}}$FERN$_{\mathcal{L}}$
FURNIVALS
ENGLAND   **Royal**
                 V.B. $R.P.C.O\,M.L.N$ R. POOLE $R.Shaws$

   j   k   l   m   n

(j) COBRIDGE, Great Britain. Circa 1890. (k) EAST LIVERPOOL, Ohio, U.S.A. Vodrey Brothers. Circa 1875. (l) CINCINNATI, Ohio, U.S.A. Rookwood Pottery Factory. Est. 1886. (m) BURSLEM, Great Britain. Fayence. Late 18th and early 19th centuries. (n) BURSLEM, Great Britain. Staffordshire. Impressed. 1735.

Rubelles
A.D.T.   RUSKIN   RUSKIN POTTERY   R.W. MARTIN & BROS.

a   b   c   d

(a) RUBELLES, France. Fayence. 1856. (b-c) WEST SMETH-
WICK, Great Britain. Pottery. 20th century. (d) GREAT BRITAIN.
R. W. Martin and Brothers. Stoneware. 1900.

Ⴑ   Ⴑ   s   Ⴑ   S   S

e   f   g   h   i   j

SECTION S
See also Section
Lines

(e) SAINT PETERSBURG, Russia. Hard paste. Painted blue. 1744.
(f-g-h-i-j) CAUGHLEY, Great Britain. Hard paste. Painted blue.
Est. 1750.

S   S   S   S   ·S   S.

k   l   m   n   o   p

(k) ROUEN, France. Fayence. Circa 1760. (l) PARIS, France. Rue
de la Roquette, factory. Souroux, potter. 1773. (m) SCHLAGGEN-
WALD, Bohemia. Hard paste. Painted. 1793-1866. (n) NYMPH-
ENBURG, Germany. Porcelain. Impressed or incised. Est. 1747.
(o) SINCENY, France. Fayence. Est. 1733. (p) SCHLAGGEN-
WALD, Bohemia. Hard paste. 1793-1866.

a   b   c   d   e   f

(a-b) SCHLAGGENWALD, Bohemia. Porcelain. 1793-1866. (c) SCHREZHEIM, Germany. Fayence. Est. 1752-1862. (d) SINCENY, France. Fayence. Painted. Est. 1733. (e) ST. CLOUD, France. Fayence, porcelain. Est. 1678-1766. (f) EISENACH, Germany. Est. 1858.

g   h   i   j   k

(g) NORD, France. St. Amand les Eaux, factory. Fayence. Est. 1718. (h) ROUEN, France. Fayence. 1760. (i) STRASBURG, Virginia, U.S.A. Samuel Bell. Impressed. Circa 1850. (j-k) SCHLESWIG, Germany. Fayence. Est. 1755.

l   m   n   o   p

(l) ST. CLOUD, France. Henri-Charles Trou, potter. Pottery and soft paste. Painted. Circa 1700. (m) SCHLESWIG, Germany. Lucke and Schmattau, founders. Fayence. 1755-1814. (n) SCHLESWIG, Germany. Fayence. 1755-1814. (o) PIRKENHAMMER, Germany. Fischer and Reichenbach. Hard paste. Impressed. 1815-1845. (p) ROUEN, France. Fayence. 1760.

a   b   c   d   e

(a) ROUEN, France. Fayence. 1760. (b) CASTELLI, Italy. 17th and 18th centuries. (c-d) SCHLESWIG. Germany. Lucke and Schmattau, founders. Fayence. 1755-1814. (e) BRISTOL, Great Britain. Joseph Flower, painter. Delft. 1739-1751.

f   g   h   i   j

(f) LA SEYNIE, France. Hard paste. Est. 1774. (g) HOLLAND T'Hart (The Stag). Fayence. Delft. 1707. (h) BUEN RETIRO, Spain. Porcelain. 1759-1808. (i) ROUEN, France. Fayence. 1760. (j) SCEAUX, France. Fayence, porcelain. 1748-1794.

k   l   m   n   o

(k) SEINE, France. Sceaux Penthievre, factory. Soft paste. 1748-1794. (l) SCHELTEN, Germany. Porcelain. Impressed. Est. 1820. (m) SCHLESWIG, Germany. Fayence. 1755-1814. (n) NEVERS, France. Jacques Seigne, painter. Fayence. Painted. 1700. (o) SCHAFFHAUSEN, Germany. Tobias Stimmer. Pottery., Painted. 16th century.

S.   S.v.E   S.E   S.E 24   SX

a   b   c   d   e

(a) GERMANY. 17th century. (b-c-d) HOLLAND. De Griekse A
(The Greek A). S. v. Eenhoorn, potter. Fayence. Delft. 1674.
(e) SEINE, France. Sceaux Penthievre, factory. Jacques Chapelle,
potter. Soft paste. 1749-1763:

SX   S.X.   ᴐℛ   Sx   Sₓ   S·X

f   g   h   i   j

(f-g-h) SEINE, France. Sceaux Penthievre, factory. Jacques Cha-
pelle, potter. Soft paste. 1749-1763. (i) CAUGHLEY, Great Britain.
Porcelain. 1750-1814. (j) SEINE, France. Sceaux, factory. Richard
Glot, potter. Fayence, soft paste. 1772-1794.

S.A. & CO.   Sadler   Sadler &   Saint-Omer
                      Green

k   l   m   n

(k) BURSLEM, Great Britain. Smith, Ambrose and Company. Staffordshire. Circa 1800. (l) LIVERPOOL, Great Britain. John Sadler,
engraver. Pottery and hard paste. Printed. 1756-1770. (m) LIVER-
POOL, Great Britain. John Sadler, engraver. Hard paste. Printed.
1756-1770. (n) SAINT OMER, France. Fayence. 1750-1780.

Salamander
Works
Woodbridge
N.J.   **SALOPIAN**   **SALT**

a   b   c

(a) WOODBRIDGE, New York, U.S.A. Salamander Works. Impressed. Circa 1875. (b) CAUGHLEY, Great Britain. Porcelain. Impressed. 1750-1814. (c) HANLEY, Great Britain. Ralph Salt, potter. Earthenware. 1820.

Samuel Troxel
Potter 1825   SAPPHO
                                             J. M. & S. CO

d   e   f

(d) MONTGOMERY COUNTY, Pennsylvania, U.S.A. Troxel Pottery. 1825. (e) SARREGUEMINES, France. Fayence. Est. 1770-19th century. (f) TRENTON, New Jersey, U.S.A. John Moses and Sons. Circa 1875.

S.BELL
S.BELL   STRASBURG, VA.   S. BELL & SONS   SB&S

g   h   i   • j

(g) STRASBURG, Virginia, U.S.A. Samuel Bell. Impressed. 1843-1852. (h) STRASBURG, Virginia, U.S.A. Samuel and Solomon Bell. Impressed. 1852-1882. (i) STRASBURG, Virginia, U.S.A. S. Bell and Sons. Impressed. 1882-1908. (j) SWINTON, Great Britain. Don Pottery, factory. Creamware. 1834.

Schiedam

Sceaux   *A : Klos*   *Schlesurg*   26
                                            S & Co

a   b   c   d

(a) SEINE, France. Sceaux Penthievre, factory. Soft paste. Painted
blue. 1748-1794. (b) SCHIEDAM, Holland. Fayence. 1775-1790.
(c) SCHLESWIG, Germany. Fayence. 1755-1814. (d) ISLE-
WORTH, Great Britain. Staffordshire-like ware. 1760-19th century.

SCOTT

Scott   Scott Brothers & Co.   PB   SCHOMAN
                                        A MOABIT·

e   f   g   h

(e-f) SUNDERLAND, Great Britain. Anthony Scott and family,
potters. 18th century. (g) PORTBELLO, Scotland. Cream-colored
ware, Staffordshire. Est. 1770. (h) MOABIT, Germany. Porcelain.
Blue. Est. 1835.

POTTERY
KOKUS
CHINA

S.E. HEIGHSHOE   SEMI-VITREOUS
SOMERSET   ARDMORE
O   MERCER CHINA

i   j   k   l

(i-j) SEBRING, Ohio, U.S.A. Sebring Pottery Company. Est. 1887.
(k) SOMERSET, Ohio, U.S.A. Heighshoe, owner. Impressed. Circa
1850. (l) TRENTON, New Jersey, U.S.A. Mercer Pottery Company.
Circa 1870.

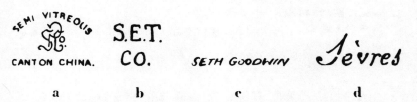

a   b   c   d

(a) STEUBENVILLE, Ohio, U.S.A. Steubenville Pottery Company. Est. 1887. (b) PITTSBURGH, Pennsylvania, U.S.A. Star Encaustic Tile Company. Est. 1882. (c) HARTFORD, Connecticut, U.S.A. Seth Goodwin. Circa 1810. (d) SEVRES, France. Soft paste, hard paste. 1793-1800.

e   f   g   h   i

(e) SEVRES, France. Soft paste, hard paste. Black for hard paste, blue for soft paste. 1941. (f) SEVRES, France. Painted black on hard paste, blue on soft paste. 1928-1940. (g-h) SEVRES, France. Soft paste, hard paste. Painted. 1792-1800. (i) EAST LIVERPOOL, Ohio, U.S.A. Sevres China Company. Est. 1900.

Sewell & Donkin   SEWELL ST. ANTHONY'S

j   k

(j) NEWCASTLE-ON-TYNE, Great Britain. Sewell and Donkin, potters. Pottery. Early 19th century. (k) NEWCASTLE-ON-TYNE, Great Britain. Sewell, potter. Impressed. Early 19th century.

Seymour & Steadman
Ravenna, O.   S&G.   Sk.U   SGIB

a   b   c   d

(a) RAVENNA, Ohio, U.S.A. Seymour and Steadman. Impressed.
Circa 1850. (b) GERMANY. Schiller and Gerbing. 1830. (c) ISLE-
WORTH, Great Britain. Joseph Shore, owner. 1760. (d) VENICE,
Italy. 1750.

                                                 SHEPLEY & SMITH
                                                   WEST TROY
S.&G ISLEWORTH   S.GREENWOOD   SHAW   N.Y.

   e   f   g   h

(e) ISLEWORTH, Great Britain. Shore and Goulding, owners. Staffordshire-like ware. Est. 1760. (f) FENTON, Great Britain. Staffordshire. Circa 1780. (g) LIVERPOOL, Great Britain. Thomas Shaw,
potter. Pottery. 1716. (h) WEST TROY, New York, U.S.A. Shepley
and Smith. Impressed. Circa 1880.

S. HOLLINS   Shore & Co.   SHORTHOSE   Shorthose & Cº

   i   j   k   l

(i) SHELTON, Great Britain. Samuel Hollins, potter. Stoneware.
Impressed. Last quarter 18th century. (j) ISLEWORTH, Great
Britain. Joseph Shore, owner. Staffordshire-like ware. 1760-19th century. (k) HANLEY, Great Britain. J. Shorthose, potter. Staffordshire. 1785-1823. (l) HANLEY, Great Britain. J. Shorthose, potter.
Black basaltes and porcelain. Impressed, printed blue. Late 18th-
19th century.

a   b   c   d

(a) HANLEY, Great Britain. Shorthose and Heath, potters. Black basaltes and porcelain. Late 18th-19th century. (b) SINCENY, France. Pottery. Painted. 1733. (c) WOMELSDORF, Pennsylvania, U.S.A. Impressed. Circa 1880. (d) EAST LIVERPOOL, Ohio, U.S.A. Smith-Phillips China Company. Late 19th century.

$Smith\ Fise\ &\ Co.$
$Manufacturers$
$Phila,$ SMITH $Soliua$ SOLOMON BELL
                   MOGADORE   STRASBURG, VA.
                   OHIO

e   f   g   h

(e) PHILADELPHIA, Pennsylvania, U.S.A. Smith, Fise and Company. Circa 1810. (f) MOGADORE, Ohio, U.S.A. J. C. Smith. Impressed. Circa 1860. (g) ALCORA, Spain. Miguel Soliva, painter. Porcelain, fayence. 1727-1750. (h) STRASBURG, Virginia, U.S.A. Samuel and Solomon Bell. Impressed. Circa 1875.

SOMERSET
POTTERY WORKS   S.PAUL   SP. CO =   SPODE.

i   j   k   l

(i) SOMERSET, Massachusetts. U.S.A. Somerset Pottery Works. Impressed. Circa 1875. (j) SAINT PAUL, France. Fayence. 18th-19th century. (k) KAOLIN, South Carolina, U.S.A. Southern Porcelain Company. Circa 1860. (l) STOKE-ON-TRENT, Great Britain. Porcelain. Impressed, painted red, blue, black, gold. 1770.

Spode

SPODₐ   *Spode*   SPODE & COPELAND

a   b   c

(a-b-c) STOKE-ON-TRENT, Great Britain. Spode, factory. Impressed or printed red, blue, black, gold. 1770-1797.

SPODE
COPELANDS CHINA   SPODE   Spode's
ENGLAND   Felspar Porcelain   Imperial

d   e   f

(d) STOKE-ON-TRENT, Great Britain. Spode, factory. Bone-porcelain. 1813-1833. (e)• STOKE-ON-TRENT, Great Britain. Spode, factory. Printed. 1770-1797. (f) STOKE-ON-TRENT, Great Britain. W. T. Copeland·and Sons. Bone-porcelain. 1833-1847.

SPODE, SON   S. PURDY   S. PURDY
& COPELAND   S. PURDY   ATWATER   PORTAGE CO.
                                          O

g   h   i   j

(g) STOKE-ON-TRENT, Great Britain. Copeland and Spode, factory. Bone-porcelain. Impressed, printed blue. 1813-1833. (h-i-j) ATWATER, Ohio, U.S.A. Solomon Purdy. Impressed. Circa 1820.

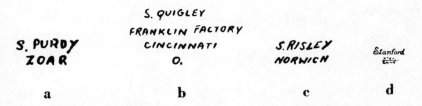

a   b   c   d

(a) ZOAR, Ohio, U.S.A. Zoar Pottery. Impressed. Circa 1845.
(b) CINCINNATI, Ohio, U.S.A. S. Quigley. Circa 1835 (doubtful
mark). (c) NORWICH, Connecticut, U.S.A. Sidney Risley. Impressed. Circa 1835. (d) LIVERPOOL, Ohio, U.S.A. Knowles,
Taylor, and Knowles. Est. 1854.

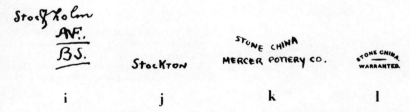

e   f   g   h

(e) STRASBURG, Virginia, U.S.A. J. S. Eberley. Impressed. 1880-
1905. (f) BURSLEM, Great Britain. Daniel Steel, potter. Blue jasper
stoneware. Impressed. 1766-1824. (g) HOLLAND. Jan Steen. Fayence. Delft. Painted blue. 1650. (h) COBRIDGE, Great Britain.
Ralph Stevenson, potter. Earthenware. 1815.

i   j   k   l

(i) RORSTRAND, Sweden. Fayence. 1725-1758. (j) SUNDER-
LAND, Great Britain. After 1800. (k) TRENTON, New Jersey,
U.S.A. Mercer Pottery Company. Est. 1869. (l) BALTIMORE,
Maryland, U.S.A. D. F. Haynes and Company. Est. 1879.

Storyhulm $\frac{22}{8.}$ *1751*
DB   *S. T. P.*   SWAN HILL
                                                       POTTERY

a   b   c

(a) RORSTRAND, Sweden. Fayence. 1725-1758. (b) MONTGOM-
ERY COUNTY, Pennsylvania, U.S.A. Samuel Troxel. Circa 1830.
(c) SOUTH AMBOY, New Jersey, U.S.A. James Carr. Impressed.
1852.

SWIANSEA   Swansea   SWANSEA   SYDNEY
                               NANGRAW

d   e   f   g

(d-e) SWANSEA, Wales. Hard paste. Stenciled red or impressed.
1814-1824. (f) NANTGARW, Wales. Swansea factory. Impressed.
1814. (g) EAST LIVERPOOL, Ohio, U.S.A. C. C. Thompson Pottery Company. Est. 1888.

SECTION T
See also Sections
Anchor, Arrow, $\mathcal{J}$. $\mathcal{J}$. $\underline{\mathcal{J}.}$ $\mathcal{F}_{b}$ $\mathcal{T}$
Lines
                          h   i   j   k   l

(h) TETTAU, Germany. Porcelain. 1794-1940. (i) TANNOWA,
Germany. Fayence, porcelain. 1813-1880. (j) KIEL, Germany. Johann Tannich, founder. Fayence. 1763-1768. (k) FRANKENTHAL,
Germany. Joseph Asam Hannong, owner. Porcelain. 1759-1762.
(l) BOW, Great Britain. Thomas Frye, manager. Porcelain. 1744-
1759.

a b c d e

(a-b) BOW, Great Britain. Thomas Frye, manager. Porcelain. 1744-1759. (c-d) HOLLAND. Antoni Ter Humpelin. Fayence. Delft. Painted blue. 1650. (e) PARIS, France. Theodore Deck. Fayence. Est. 1859.

f g h i j

(f) HOLLAND. Philip Wouvermans. Fayence. Delft. Painted blue. 1600. (g-h-i) KLOSTERLE, Germany. Porcelain, lead-glazed earthenware. 1793. (j) PREMIERES, France. Lavalle, potter. 1783.

k l m n o

(k) MOUSTIERS, France. Joseph Olery, painter. Fayence. 1721. (l) NAPLES, Italy. Late 19th century. (m) BRISTOL, Great Britain. Tebo, modeler. Porcelain. 1770-1775. (n) NEVERS, France. Tite Ristori. Pottery. Painted. 1850. (o) SCHAFFHAUSEN, Germany. Tobias Stimmer. Pottery. Painted. 1560.

𝒮.   𝒥𝒱   T.W.J.L.   Tannawa

a   b   c   d

(a) NEVERS, France. Fayence. 18th century. (b) LIONVILLE, Pennsylvania, U.S.A. T. Vickers. 1805. (c) SOUTH AMBOY, New Jersey, U.S.A. Warne and Letts. 1806. (d) TANNOWA, Bohemia. Fayence, porcelain. 1813-1880.

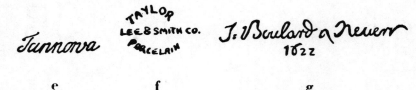

e   f   g

(e) TANNOWA, Bohemia. Fayence, porcelain. 1813-1880. (f) EAST LIVERPOOL, Ohio, U.S.A. Taylor, Smith, and Taylor Company. Est. 1900. (g) NEVERS, France. Fayence. 1622.

T. CRAFTS & SON
WHATELY
MASS.   Tetschen   TEXAS   T. FELL & CO.

h   i   j   k

(h) WHATELEY, Massachusetts, U.S.A. Crafts, Thomas and El-bridge. Impressed. Circa 1830. (i) BODENBACH, Germany. 1829. (j) EAST LIVERPOOL, Ohio, U.S.A. Cartwright Brothers. 1890. (k) NEWCASTLE, Great Britain. Thomas Fell, potter. 1817.

T FERESCH   T. FLETCHER & CO.   T. G. BOONE + SONS POTTERS
                                          NAVY ST BROOKLYN

a   b   c

(a) KLUM, Germany. Porcelain. Circa 1800. (b) SHELTON, Great
Britain. Fletcher, owner. Staffordshire. 18th century. (c) BROOK-
LYN, New York, U.S.A. T. G. Boone. Circa 1845.

T. GREEN   T. HAIG   T. HARLEY   t'hart
                                   Lane End

d   e   f   g

(d) FENTON, Great Britain. Staffordshire. 1830-1849. (e) PHILA-
DELPHIA, Pennsylvania, U.S.A. Thomas Haig. 1850. (f) LANE
END, Great Britain. Staffordshire. Impressed. 1809. (g) HOL-
LAND. T'Hart (The Stag). Fayence. Delft. Painted blue. 1764.

          THE EDWARD NORTON CO,
          BENNINGTON, VT.

h   i   j

(h) EAST LIVERPOOL, Ohio, U.S.A. United States Pottery Company. Est. 1846. (i) BENNINGTON, Vermont, U.S.A. Edward Norton and Company. Impressed. 1886-1894. (j) HOLLAND. Fayence.
Delft. 1730.

a   b   c

(a) HAVILAND, France. Painted red, green. 1914. (b) HAVI-
LAND, France. Whiteware. Printed green. 1920-1936. (c) HAVI-
LAND, France. Decorated ware. Printed red. 1920.

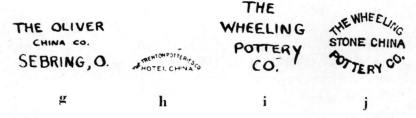

d   e   f

(d) HAVILAND, France. Decorated ware. Printed red. 1926. (e)
NEW YORK, New York, U.S.A. Haviland, company. Printed green,
black. 1936. (f) NEW YORK, New York, U.S.A. Haviland, company. Printed dark red, black. After 1937.

THE OLIVER
CHINA CO.
SEBRING, O.   TRENTON POTTERIES CO. HOTEL CHINA

THE
WHEELING
POTTERY
CO.

THE WHEELING
STONE CHINA
POTTERY CO.

g   h   i   j

(g) SEBRING, Ohio, U.S.A. Oliver China Company. Est. 1899.
(h) TRENTON, New Jersey, U.S.A. Trenton Potteries Company.
Est. 1865. (i-j) WHEELING, West Virginia, U.S.A. Wheeling Pottery Company. Est. 1879.

Thomas

THOMAS AND WILLIAM SANS — China Co. — THOMAS DAWSON & CO. — Thomas Harris

a   b   c   d

(a) GREAT BRITAIN. Thomas and William Sans, potters. Slip-ware. 1707. (b) EAST LIVERPOOL, Ohio, U.S.A. C. C. Thompson Pottery Company. Est. 1888. (c) SUNDERLAND, Great Britain. Thomas Dawson, potter. Circa 1850. (d) CUYAHOGA FALLS, Ohio, U.S.A. Thomas Harris. Impressed. Est. 1863.

THOMAS TOFT   THOMAS SHARPE   Thos Furnival & Sons Cobridge Staffore   T&J HOLLINS

e   f   g   h

(e) BURSLEM, Great Britain. Thomas Toft, potter. Slipware. 1670. (f) GREAT BRITAIN. Thomas Sharpe, potter. Circa 1830. (g) COBRIDGE, Great Britain. Thomas Furnival. After 1850. (h) HANLEY, Great Britain. Hollins, potter. Stoneware. Impressed. Circa 1820.

T., J. & J. MAYER   T. Johnson   T. Mayer   T. O. GOODWIN HARTFORD

i   j   k   l

(i) HANLEY, Great Britain. Thomas, John, Joseph Mayer, potters. After 1836. (j) GREAT BRITAIN. T. Johnson, potter. Slipware. 1694. (k) STOKE-ON-TRENT, Great Britain. Fayence. Impressed. 1820. (l) HARTFORD, Connecticut, U.S.A. Thomas Goodwin. Circa 1850.

Tomlinson & Co.   TOULOUSE   T. P. Co.   T. READ
                                           CHINA

a   b   c   d

(a) FERRYBRIDGE, Great Britain. W. Tomlinson, potter. 18th-
19th century. (b) TOULOUSE, France. Fayence. Early 19th century. (c) TRENTON, New Jersey, U.S.A. Trenton Pottery Company. Circa 1870. (d) NEWPORT, Ohio, U.S.A. Thomas Read.
Impressed. Circa 1860.

T. READ   TRENTON CHINA CO.   TRENTON POTTERIES Co.
TUSCARAWAS CO.   TRENTON, N.J.   TRENTON, NEW JERSEY
                                           USA

e   f   g

(e) NEWPORT, Ohio, U.S.A. Thomas Read. Impressed. 1850-1865.
(f) TRENTON, New Jersey, U.S.A. Trenton China Company.
1860-1890. (g) TRENTON, New Jersey, U.S.A. Trenton Potteries
Company. Est. 1865.

TRENT TILE
TRENTON, N.J   J.M.&S.CO.   J.M.&S.CO.   T. SHARPE   T. SNEYD
U.S.A.

h   i   j   k   l

(h) TRENTON, New Jersey, U.S.A. Trenton Tile Company. 1885.
(i-j) TRENTON, New Jersey, U.S.A. John Moses and Sons. Circa
1875. (k) GREAT BRITAIN. Thomas Sharpe, potter. 1821-1838.
(l) HANLEY, Great Britain. T. Sneyd, potter. Staffordshire. Impressed. 1800.

Tucker & Hulme
China Manufacturers
Philadelphia
1825

Tucker & Hulme.
Philadelphia
1825

TURADO
WELLER

TURNER

TURNER

a   b   c   d   e

(a-b) PHILADELPHIA, Pennsylvania, U.S.A. Tucker and Hulme.
Est. 1825. (c) ZANESVILLE, Ohio, U.S.A. S. A. Weller. Late 19th
century. (d) CAUGHLEY, Great Britain. Porcelain. 1750. (e)
CAUGHLEY, Great Britain. Hard paste, fayence. Impressed. 1772.

$\widetilde{Juyn}$ T. WETHERILL   TWIGG

f   g   h

(f) HOLLAND. De Porceleyne Schootel (The Porcelain Dish).
Fayence. Delft. 1764. (g) LAMBETH, Great Britain. Delft. 19th
century. (h) SWINTON, Great Britain. Pottery. 1750.

U & C

U
DALWITZ

UPTON BELL
WAYNESBORO, PA.

SECTION U
See also Sections
V, W, Lines,
Shield

i   j   k

(i) SARREGUEMINES, France. Fayence, porcelain. Est. 1770.
(j) DALLWITZ, Germany. Est. 1804. (k) WAYNESBORO, Pennsylvania, U.S.A. Upton Bell. Impressed. Circa 1895.

SECTION V
See also Sections
U, W, X-Y, Lines,
Shield

a   b   c   d   e   f

(a) VENICE, Italy. Nathaniel Hewelcke, potter. Porcelain. Incised.
1757-1763. (b) VIANNA DO CASTELLO, Portugal. Fayence. Est.
1774. (c) HOLLAND. De Drie Klokken (The Three Bells). Fayence. Delft. 1675. (d) VIANNA DO CASTELLO, Portugal. Fayence. Est. 1774. (e) VARAGES, France. Fayence. 18th century.
(f) LIONVILLE, Pennsylvania, U.S.A. T. and J. Vickers. 1806.

g   h   i   j   k

(g) VARAGES, France. Fayence. 18th century. (h) VINOVO,
Italy. Porcelain. Underglaze blue or incised. Est. 1776. (i) VENICE,
Italy. Francesco and Giuseppe Vezzi, porcelain makers. Porcelain.
Painted blue. 1719-1740. (j) VISTA ALEGRE, Portugal. Hard
paste. Est. 1824. (k) ALCORA, Spain. Porcelain, fayence. Est. 1750.

l   m   n   o   p

(l) STRASBURG, France. Valentin Gusi, modeler. Porcelain. Circa
1750. (m) ROUEN, France. Jacques Dubois, potter. 1783. (n-o)
HOLLAND. Jan van der Kloot. Fayence. Delft. Painted blue. 1764.
(p) HOLLAND. De Metale Pot (The Metal Pot). Fayence. Delft.
1691.

a   b   c   d   e   f

(a) HOLLAND. De Metale Pot (The Metal Pot). Fayence. Delft.
1691. (b-c) HOLLAND. De Dubbelde Schenkkan (The Double
Jug). Fayence. Delft. 1689. (d) NIDERVILLER, France. Baron
Jean-Louis Beyerle, owner. Fayence. 1754-1770. (e) VINOVO,
Italy. Porcelain. Est. 1776. (f) HOLLAND. De Drie Klokken (The
Three Bells). Fayence. Delft. 1675.

g   h   i   j   k

(g-h) MARSEILLES, France. Veuve Perrin, potter. Fayence.
Painted black. 1790. (i) FAENZA, Italy. Calamelli Virgiliotto,
potter and painter. Fayence. 1570. (j) FRANKENTHAL, Germany.
Hard paste. Est. 1755-1799. (k) METTLACH, Germany. Fayence.
19th century.

l   m   n   o

(l) ASHFIELD, Massachusetts, U.S.A. Van Horn and Boyden.
Impressed. Circa 1855. (m-n-o) METTLACH, Germany. Fayence,
glazed earthenware. Est. 1809.

a   b   c   d

(a) HOLLAND. De Porceleyne Schootel (The Porcelain Dish).
Fayence. Delft. 1764. (b) BUEN RETIRO, Spain. Hard paste. 1759-
1808. (c) PARIS, France. Rue Thiroux, factory. Hard paste. 1775.
(d) VENICE, Italy. Hard paste. Painted red, blue. 1700.

e   f   g   h

(e) VENICE, Italy. Hard paste. Painted blue. 1719. (f) SEBRING,
Ohio, U.S.A. Oliver China Company. Est. 1899. (g) STRASBURG,
France. Hard paste. 1729-1771. (h) VIENNA, Austria. Hard paste.
1770.

J. M. & S. CO.   VILLEROY & BOCH

i   j   k   l

(i) TRENTON, New Jersey, U.S.A. Glasgow Pottery Company.
Circa 1875. (j) METTLACH, Germany. Villeroy and Boch, potters.
Fayence. 1842. (k) EAST LIVERPOOL, Ohio, U.S.A. Knowles,
Taylor, and Knowles. Est. 1854. (l) COBRIDGE, Great Britain.
Staffordshire. Impressed. 1773.

a   b   c   d   e

(a) BERLIN, Germany. Wegeley, founder. Hard paste. Painted blue. 1751. (b) THURINGIA, Germany. Wallendorf,factory. Porcelain. Est. 1764. (c) PLYMOUTH, Great Britain. Hard paste. Painted blue. 1768. (d) BORDEAUX, France. Porcelain. Painted gold, underglaze blue. 1781. (e) WEESP, Holland. Porcelain. Est. 1759.

f   g   h   i   j

(f) PLYMOUTH, Great Britain. Hard paste. Painted red, blue, gold. 1768. (g) BUDWEIS, Germany. Porcelain. Circa 1820. (h) BERLIN, Germany. Wegeley, founder. Hard paste. Painted blue. 1751. (i) BUDWEIS, Germany. Porcelain. Circa 1820. (j) STOKE-ON-TRENT, Great Britain. Thomas Wolfe, potter. Impressed. 18th-19th century.

k   l   m   n   o

(k-l) WORCESTER, Great Britain. Hard paste. Est. 1751. (m) WARSAW, Poland. Wolff, potter. 1783. (n) WORCESTER, Great Britain. Hard paste. Est. 1751. (o) WALLENDORF, Germany. Painted blue. Est. 1764.

a　　　　b　　　　c　　　　d　　　　e.

(a) ROUEN, France. Fayence. 1720. (b-c) WORCESTER, Great
Britain. Hard paste. Est. 1751. (d) PHILADELPHIA, Pennsyl-
vania, U.S.A. Joseph Hemphill. Circa 1835. (e) BERLIN, Germany.
Wegeley, founder. Porcelain. 1751.

f　　　　g　　　h　　　i　　　j

(f-g-h) WALLENDORF, Germany. Porcelain. Painted blue. Est.
1764. (i) HOLLAND. De Oude Moriaan's Hooft (The Old Moor's
Head). Fayence. Delft. 1661. (j) WIESBADEN, Germany. Fayence. Est. 1770.

k　　　l　　　m　　　n　　　o

(k) ROUEN, France. Michel Vallet, potter. Fayence. 1757 (l) APT,
France. Fayence. Est. 1728. (m) COBRIDGE, Great Britain. W.
Brownfield, potter. 1836. (n) HOLLAND. De Drie Klokken (The
Three Bells). Fayence. Delft. 1764. (o) BERLIN, Germany. Wege-
ley, founder. Porcelain. 1751.

W. F.   a   b   c   d   e

(a) BRISTOL, Great Britain. Pottery. 1853. (b) CHELSEA, Great Britain. Porcelain. 1745-1784. (c) HOLLAND. De Drie Porceleyne Fleschen (The Three Porcelain Bottles). Fayence. Delft. 1697. (d) HOLLAND. Fayence. Delft. 1663. (e) WORCESTER, Great Britain. Porcelain. Est. 1751.

W PC   W:V:B   W.V.D.   W.V.D.B $\overline{S}$

f   g   h   i   j

(f) WORCESTER, Great Britain. Hard paste. Est. 1751. (g) HOLLAND. De Twee Wildemans (The Two Savages). Fayence. Delft. 1750. (h) HOLLAND. De Boot (The Boat). Fayence. Delft. 1707. (i) HOLLAND. De Fortuyn (The Fortune). Fayence. Delft. 1764. (j) HOLLAND. De Fortuyn (The Fortune). Fayence. Delft. 1759.

W. W   W ᗈ   W.ABSOLON, YARM.   W. Adams

k   l   m   n

(k) GREAT BRITAIN. Slipware. 1749. (l) HOLLAND. De Boot (The Boat). Fayence. Delft. 1707. (m) YARMOUTH, Great Britain. Absolon, enameler. Circa 1800. (n) TUNSTALL, Great Britain. William Adams. Pottery. Impressed. 1805.

W. ADAMS & Co.   W. ADAMS & SONS   W. ADAMS & SONS
STOKE.UPON.TRENT

a   b   c

(a) TUNSTALL, Great Britain. William Adams, potter. Pottery.
Impressed. 1787. (b) STOKE-ON-TRENT, Great Britain. W.
Adams, potter. Circa 1825. (c) STOKE-ON-TRENT, Great Britain.
W. Adams, potter. Pottery. Impressed. Circa 1850.

WAGONER BROS.
VANPORT
PA.   W.A.GRAY & SONS   WAIT & RICKETTS
                                     SPRINGFIELD, O.

d   e   f

(d) VANPORT, Pennsylvania, U.S.A. Wagoner Brothers. Impressed. Circa 1865. (e) PORTBELLO, Scotland. Est. 1770 (f)
SPRINGFIELD, Ohio, U.S.A. Wait and Ricketts. Impressed. Circa
1870.

WALDORF   WALTER ORCUTT & CO.   WARNE
MERCER CHINA   ASHFIELD, MASS.   Walton   S.AMBOY
                                                   N.JERSEY

g   h   i   j

(g) TRENTON, New Jersey, U.S.A. Mercer Pottery Company. Est.
1868. (h) ASHFIELD, Massachusetts, U.S.A. Walter Orcutt and
Company. Impressed. Circa 1850. (i) BURSLEM, Great Britain.
John Walton, potter. Earthernware. 18th-19th century. (j) SOUTH
AMBOY, New Jersey, U.S.A. Thomas Warne. Circa 1800.

WARNE & LETTS
S. AMBOY
N. JERSY

WARWICK
-SEMI-
PORCELAIN

WASHINGTON
KTOK
CHINA

W. & B.

a   b   c   d

(a) SOUTH AMBOY, New Jersey, U.S.A. Warne and Letts. Circa 1805. (b) WHEELING, West Virginia, U.S.A. Warwick China Company. Est. 1887. (c) EAST LIVERPOOL, Ohio, U.S.A. Knowles, Taylor, and Knowles. Est. 1854. (d) WEDGWOOD, Great Britain. Wedgwood and Bentley. Earthernware. 1769-1780.

W B&S

W. BULLOCK
ROSEVILLE, O.

W. BURTON
CODNOR PARK

W. DIXON

e   f   g   h

(e) COBRIDGE, Great Britain. W. Brownfield, potter. 1836. (f) ROSEVILLE, Ohio, U.S.A. W. Bullock. Impressed. Circa 1875. (g) GREAT BRITAIN. W. Burton. 1821-30. (h) SUNDERLAND, Great Britain. W. Dixon, potter. 18th-19th century.

WEBSTER & SEYMOUR
HARTFORD

Wedgwood

WEDGWOOD

Wedgwood &
Bentley

i   j   k   l

(i) HARTFORD, Connecticut, U.S.A. Webster and Seymour. Impressed. 1857-1873. (j) ETRURIA, Great Britain. Wedgwood, factory. Pottery. Impressed. 1771. (k) ETRURIA, Great Britain. Wedgwood, factory. Pottery, porcelain. Impressed on pottery, 1771; printed red, blue, gold on porcelain, 1812-1816. (l) ETRURIA, Great Britain. Wedgwood, factory. Wedgwood and Bentley, owners. Pottery. Incised. 1769-1780.

Wedgwood & Co.

WEDGWOOD ENGLAND

𝖶𝖤𝖣𝖦𝖶𝖮𝖮𝖣 & CO   Ferrybridge

a   b   c

(a-b) FERRYBRIDGE, Great Britain. Ralph Wedgwood, owner.
Stoneware, cream-colored ware. Impressed. 1796-1800. (c) ETRU-
RIA, Great Britain. Wedgwood, factory. Pottery. After 1891.

Wedgwood
Eturia
England   Wedgwood & Sons   Z
                                          WEDGWOOD 𝖜𝖩

d   e   f

(d) ETRURIA, Great Britain. Wedgwood, factory. Pottery. After
1891. (e) ETRURIA, Great Britain. Wedgwood, factory. Pottery.
1790. (f) ETRURIA, Great Britain. Wedgwood, factory. Pottery.
Impressed. After 1780.

WEEKS, COOK,   W.E.P.CO.   WEST END
& WEEKS   CHINA   POTTERY CO.   WHITE & WOOD

g   h   i   j

(g) AKRON, Ohio, U.S.A. Weeks, Cook, and Weeks. Circa 1882.
(h-i) EAST LIVERPOOL, Ohio, U.S.A. West End Pottery Company. Est. 1893. (j) BINGHAMTON, New York, U.S.A. White and
Wood. Impressed. 1850.

W. H. Lehew & Co.
Strasburg, VA   WIEN   WIENER   WILLIAM AND
                                                GEORGE TAYLOR

a   b   c   d

(a) STRASBURG, Virginia, U.S.A. Lehew and Company. Impressed. Est. 1885. (b-c) BUDWEIS, Germany. Porcelain. 1818. (d) GREAT BRITAIN. William and George Taylor. Slipware. 1707.

Williams & Reppert   William Ellis Tucker
   Greensboro   China Manufacturer
      PA.   Philadelphia   WILLIAM • SANS
                                 1825

e   f   g

(e) GREENSBORO, Pennsylvania, U.S.A. Williams and Peppert. Impressed, blue. Circa 1875. (f) PHILADELPHIA, Pennsylvania, U.S.A. W. E. Tucker. Overglaze. After 1826. (g) BURSLEM, Great Britain. Staffordshire. Impressed. 1670.

William • Jalon   WINCANTON   WOLFE & HAMILTON
                                        STOKE

h   i   j

(h) GREAT BRITAIN. Slipware. Circa 1675. (i) BRISTOL, Great Britain. Wincanton, factory. Earthernware. Est. 17th century. (j) STOKE-ON-TRENT, Great Britain. Wolfe and Hamilton, potters. Painted red. 18th-19th century.

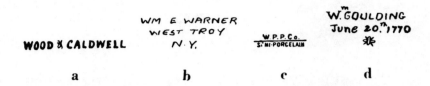

WM E WARNER
WEST TROY
WOOD ※ CALDWELL   N·Y. $\overline{\underset{\text{S. MI-PORCELAIN}}{\text{W P.P.Co.}}}$ W͞.GOULDING
June 20.ⁿ1770

a   b   c   d

(a) BURSLEM, Great Britain. Staffordshire. Impressed. 1790.
(b) WEST TROY, New York, U.S.A. William Warner. Circa 1850.
(c) WELLSVILLE, Ohio, U.S.A. Pioneer Pottery Company. Est.
1879. (d) ISLEWORTH, Great Britain. Richard and William
Goulding, potters. Slipware. 1760.

WOLFE & HAMILTON
W.MARTEEN   STOKE   WOMELSDORF   WOOD
POTTER
DAYTON
O.

e   f   g   h

(e) PENNSYLVANIA, U.S.A. W. Marteen. Circa 1875. . (f)
STOKE-ON-TRENT, Great Britain. Wolfe and Hamilton, potters.
18th-19th century. (g) WOMELSDORF, Pennsylvania, U.S.A. Willoughby Smith. Impressed. 1864-1905. (h) DAYTON, Ohio, U.S.A.
Wood. Impressed. Circa 1870.

Woronzou and Co.   W.RICH   W.SMITH   W.S. & Coˢ
Wedgewood

i   j   k   l

(i) LIANELLY, Wales. Earthenware. Circa 1870. (j) GREAT
BRITAIN. W. Rich, potter. Slipware. 1700. (k) WOMELSDORF,
Pennsylvania, U.S.A. Willoughby Smith. Impressed. 1864-1905. (l)
STOCKTON-ON-TEES, Great Britain. William Smith and Com-
pany. Cream-colored ware. 1826-1848.

W.S.MAYERS
ROSEVILLE   W.STEVENSON   ᵓ·ᵇ/·⁄ᵉ⁻˃˃⁺   W.W.L.   Wyoming
OHIO   HANLEY   ᵂⁱⁱ'ᵉ˸˸   DALWITZ

a   b   c   d   e

(a) ROSEVILLE, Ohio, U.S.A. W. S. Mayers. Painted blue. Circa 1870. (b) HANLEY, Great Britain. Circa 1820. (c) HOLLAND. Willem van der Velde, artist. Fayence. Delft. Painted color. 1660. (d) DALLWITZ, Bohemia. W. W. Lorenz. Cream-colored earthenware. 1832. (e) EAST LIVERPOOL, Ohio, U.S.A. Knowles, Taylor and Knowles. Est. 1854.

XX   XX   XE   Y   'YoiKmAR   SECTION X-Y
                                                                 See also Sections
f   g   h   i   j   V, W, Lines

(f-g) VAUX, France. Hard paste. 1769; or BORDEAUX, France. Porcelain. 1781-87. (h) HOLLAND. De Griekse A (The Greek A). Fayence. Delft. 1674. (i) THURINGIA, Germany. Rudolstadt, factory. Hard paste. Painted color. 1758. (j) BEDFORD, New York, U.S.A. Leon Volkmar. 1930.

Z   Z   ZR   Z:DEX   ZOAR   SECTION Z
                                                               See also Section
k   l   m   n   o   Lines

(k-l-m) ZURICH, Switzerland. Pottery, hard paste. Painted blue. After 1763. (n) HOLLAND. De Drie Astonne (The Three Ash Barrels). Fayence. Delft. 1720. (o) ZOAR, Ohio, U.S.A. Zoar Pottery. Impressed. Circa 1850.

SECTION **ANCHOR**
See also Sections
Arrow, Lines

a   b   c   d   e   f

(a) LEEDS, Great Britain. Cream-colored ware. Painted. Est. 1760.
(b) HOLLAND. De Ster (The Star). Fayence. Delft. 1705. (c-d)
SCEAUX, France. Pottery, soft paste. Painted blue. 1748. (e-f)
CHELSEA, Great Britain. Soft paste. Painted gold, red, brown,
purple. 1745-1784.

g   h   i   j   k   l

(g) WORCESTER, Great Britain. Painted red. Est. 1751. (h-i)
CHELSEA, Great Britain. Soft paste. Painted red or gold. 1745-
1784. (j) SCEAUX, France. Pottery, soft paste. Painted blue. 1784.
(k-l) CHELSEA, Great Britain. Porcelain. 1745-1784.

m   n   o   p   q   r

(m) CHELSEA, Great Britain. Porcelain. 1745-1784. (n) SCEAUX,
France. Fayence, porcelain. After 1775. (o) METTLACH, Germany. Glazed earthenware. Est. 1809. (p) POPPELSDORF, Germany. Fayence. Impressed. Est. 1755. (q-r) CHELSEA, Great
Britain. Soft paste. Painted gold, red. 1745-1784.

a   b   c   d   e   f

(**a**) SAVONA, Italy. Fayence. 17th-18th century. (**b-c**) CHELSEA, Great Britain. Porcelain. Underglaze blue, gold. 1750-1769. (**d**) DERBY, Great Britain. Porcelain. 1770-1780. (**e**) CHELSEA, Great Britain. Porcelain. Underglaze blue, gold. 1750-1769. (**f**) BUEN RETIRO, Spain. Soft paste. 1759-1808.

g   h   i   j   k   l

(**g**) VENICE, Italy. Hard paste. Painted red. 1765. (**h**) BOW, Great Britain. Hard paste. Painted red, blue. Est. 1744. (**i**) CHELSEA, Great Britain. Porcelain. Underglaze blue, gold. 1750-1769. (**j**) CINCINNATI, Ohio, U.S.A. Rookwood Pottery Company. 1890. (**k-l**) CHELSEA, Great Britain. Soft paste. Painted gold, red. 1745.

m   n   o   p   q

(**m-n**) CHELSEA, Great Britain. Soft paste. Painted gold, red. 1745-1784. (**o**) COLOGNE, Germany. Eugen Cremer, potter. Pottery. Painted blue. 1800. (**p-q**) BOW, Great Britain. Soft paste. Painted red, brown. 1760-1780.

a   b   c   d   e

(a) CHELSEA, Great Britain. Soft paste. Painted gold, red. 1745-1784. (b) BOW, Great Britain. Soft paste. Painted red, blue, brown. 1760-1780. (c) CHELSEA, Great Britain. Soft paste. 1745-1784. (d-e) BOW, Great Britain. Soft paste. Painted red, brown. 1760-1780.

f   g   h   i

(f-g-h-i) BOW, Great Britain. Soft paste. Painted red, blue, brown. 1760-1780.

j   k   l   m   n   o

(j) BOW, Great Britain. Porcelain. 1745-1770. (k-l-m) CHELSEA, Great Britain. Soft paste. Underglaze blue, red, blue, purple. 1749-1756. (n) DERBY, Great Britain. Soft paste. Painted gold, lilac, red. 1777. (o) GERMANY. Circa 1870.

a   b   c   d   e

(a) TRENTON, New Jersey, U.S.A. Anchor Pottery Company.
Printed. Circa 1895. (b) BOW, Great Britain. Porcelain. 1745-1770.
(c) SHROPSHIRE, Great Britain. Coalport or Coalbrookdale factory. Porcelain. Painted blue. Est. 1799. (d) FENTON, Great Britain. Impressed. 1845. (e) DERBY-CHELSEA, Great Britain. Soft
paste. Painted gold or red. 1770.

f   g   h   i   j

(f) DERBY-CHELSEA, Great Britain. Porcelain. Painted blue,
lilac, gold. 1770. (g) LONGPORT, Great Britain. John Davenport,
potter. Earthenware, porcelain. 1793-1882. (h) LONGPORT, Great
Britain. John Davenport, potter. Earthenware, porcelain. Impressed. 1793-1882. (i) DERBY, Great Britain. Porcelain. 1745.
(j) NEWCASTLE, Great Britain. Thomas Fell, potter. Impressed.
18th-19th century.

k   l   m   n   o

(k) FAENZA, Italy. 1850. (l) NEUHOLDENSLEBEN, Germany.
Hubbe Brothers. Circa 1875. (m) VENICE, Italy. Giovanni Mar-
cone. Soft paste. Painted gold, color. 1700. (n) GUSTAFSBERG,
Sweden. Fayence. 1786-1797. (o) VENICE, Italy. Porcelain.
Painted red. 1765-1811.

a   b   c   d   e

(a) LIMOGES, France. Porcelain. 1842-1898. (b) LIVERPOOL,
Great Britain. Cream-colored earthenware. 1793-1841. (c) LONG-
PORT, Great Britain. John Davenport, potter. Earthenware, porce-
lain. Impressed. 1793-1882. (d) CALDAS, Portugal. Mafra, maker.
Pottery. Impressed. 1800. (e) MIDDLESBOROUGH, Great Britain.
Pottery. Printed or impressed. 1800.

f   g   h   i   j

(f) CHELSEA, Great Britain. Porcelain. Underglaze blue, purple,
blue. 1752-1756. (g) BOW, Great Britain. Porcelain. 1745-1770.
(h) LONGTON, Great Britain. 19th century. (i) SEINE, France.
Sceaux, factory. Porcelain, fayence. 1748-1794. (j) SEINE, France.
Sceaux, factory. Porcelain, fayence. 1775.

k   l   m   n   o

(k-l) WORCESTER, Great Britain. Richard Holdship, decorator.
Hard paste. Painted color. 1756-1774. (m) COBRIDGE, Great Britain. After 1891. (n) TRENTON, New Jersey, U.S.A. Thomas Maddock and Sons. Est. 1882. (o) BUEN RETIRO, Spain. Soft paste.
1759-1808.

SECTION **ANIMAL
AND FISH**
See also Sections
**Circle and Sign,
Crown and Shield,
Shield, Square**

a   b   c   d

(a) DEDHAM, Massachusetts, U.S.A. Dedham Pottery Company.
1897. (b) FURSTENBERG, Germany. Porcelain. Est. 1747. (c)
HESSE CASSEL, Germany. Hard paste. Painted blue. 1763. (d)
OIRON, France. 16th century.

e   f   g   h   i

(e-f) AMSTERDAM, Holland. Hard paste. Painted blue 1772. (g)
FRANKENTHAL, Bavaria. Hard paste. Painted blue. 1754. (h)
SYRACUSE, New York, U.S.A. Onondaga Pottery Company. Est.
1871. (i) TRENTON, New Jersey, U.S.A. Fell and Thropp Company. 19th century.

j   k   l   m

(j-k) SAN FRANCISCO, California, U.S.A. Irelan Linna. Est. 1899.
(l-m) SWINTON, Great Britain. Rockingham, factory. Hard paste.
Painted red. 1824.

E. BRAIN & CO., LTD.   SEMI-GRANITE.   HC

    a   b   c   d

(a) STOKE-ON-TRENT, Great Britain. Foley China, E. Brain and Company. Porcelain. 20th century. (b) EAST LIVERPOOL, Ohio, U.S.A. Taylor, Smith and Taylor Company. Est. 1899. (c) EAST LIVERPOOL, Ohio, U.S.A. C. C. Thompson Pottery Company. Est. 1888. (d) HESSE CASSEL, Germany. Hard paste. Underglaze blue. 1763.

    e   f

(e) EAST LIVERPOOL, Ohio, U.S.A. Knowles, Taylor, and Knowles. Est. 1854. (f) BUFFALO, New York, U.S.A. Buffalo Pottery Company. Circa 1905.

   g   h   i   j

(g) TUNSTALL, Great Britain. Printed. After 1891. (h) SWINTON, Great Britain. Don Pottery. Printed, impressed. 19th century. (i) IRELAND. Belleek, factory. Painted color. Circa 1860. (j) BURSLEM, Great Britain. Ralph Wedgwood, owner. Cream-colored ware. 1796-1800.

a   b   c   d

(**a**) GERMANY, Lorenz Hutschenreuther. Hard paste. Est. 1864.
(**b**) STOKE-ON-TRENT, Great Britain. S. Fielding and Company.
19th century. (**c**) LONGTON, Great Britain. 19th century. (**d**)
EAST LIVERPOOL, Ohio, U.S.A. East End Pottery Company. 19th
century.

e   f   g   h

(**e**) BEAVER FALLS, Pennsylvania, U.S.A. Est. 1881. (**f**)
PHOENIXVILLE, Pennsylvania, U.S.A. Est. 1894. (**g**) LIVER-
POOL, Ohio, U.S.A. John Goodwin. Est. 1844. (**h**) STEUBEN-
VILLE, Ohio, U.S.A. Steubenville Pottery Company. Est. 1879.

i   j   k   l

(**i-j-k**) EAST LIVERPOOL, Ohio, U.S.A. Vodrey Brothers. Circa
1875. (**l**) WORCESTER, Great Britain. Hard paste. 1820-1840.

a   b   c   d

(a) WELLSVILLE, Ohio, U.S.A. Pioneer Pottery Company. Circa 1890. (b) TRENTON, New Jersey, U.S.A. American Crockery Company. Est. 1876. (c) TRENTON, New Jersey, U.S.A. Prospect Hill Pottery Company. Est. 1880. (d) TRENTON, New Jersey, U.S.A. Glasgow Pottery Company. Circa 1880.

e   f   g   h

(e) TRENTON, New Jersey, U.S.A. Glasgow Pottery Company. Circa 1880. (f) JERSEY CITY, New Jersey, U.S.A. Rouse. and Turner. Est. 1875. (g) PEORIA, Illinois, U.S.A. Peoria Pottery Company. Circa 1880. (h) TRENTON, New Jersey, U.S.A. Empire Pottery Company. 1875.

i   j   k   l

(i) EVANSVILLE, Indiana, U.S.A. Crown Pottery Company. Est. 1891. (j) NEW YORK, New York, U.S.A. New York City Pottery Company. Circa 1875. (k) TRENTON, New Jersey, U.S.A. East Trenton Pottery Company. Est. 1888. (l) EAST LIVERPOOL, Ohio, U.S.A. East End Pottery Company. 19th century.

a   b   c

(a) SHELTON, Great Britain. After 1850. (b) TUNSTALL, Great Britain. Est. 1881. (c) BURSLEM, Great Britain. 18th-19th century.

d   e   f   g

(d) TRENTON, New Jersey, U.S.A. Glasgow Pottery Company. Circa 1875. (e) TRENTON, New Jersey, U.S.A. Ott and Brewer. Circa 1880. (f) WHEELING, West Virginia, U.S.A. Wheeling Pottery Company. Est. 1879. (g) STEUBENVILLE, Ohio, U.S.A. Steubenville Pottery Company. Est. 1879.

h   i   j   k

(h) BURSLEM, Great Britain. T. and R. Boote. Late 18th century. (i) EAST LIVERPOOL, Ohio, U.S.A. William Brunt Pottery Company. Circa 1875. (j) TORONTO, Ohio, U.S.A. American China Company. Est. 1897. (k) CINCINNATI, Ohio, U.S.A. Brockman Pottery Company. Est. 1863.

a   b   c   d

(a) ELIZABETH, New Jersey, U.S.A. L. B. Beerbower (Beerbauer) Company. Impressed. After 1880. (b) TRENTON, New Jersey, U.S.A. Glasgow Pottery Company. 1875. (c) TRENTON, New Jersey, U.S.A. Ott and Brewer. Circa 1875. (d) TRENTON. New Jersey, Prospect Hill Pottery Company. Est. 1880.

e   f   g   h

(e) TRENTON, New Jersey, U.S.A. Prospect Hill Pottery Company. Est. 1880. (f) TRENTON, New Jersey, U.S.A. Willetts Manufacturing Company. Est. 1880. (g-h) PEORIA, Illinois, U.S.A. Peoria Pottery Company. Circa 1885.

i   j   k   l

(i) TRENTON, New Jersey, U.S.A. Fell and Thropp Company. 19th century. (j) TRENTON, New Jersey, U.S.A. East Trenton Pottery Company. Est. 1888. (k) TRENTON, New Jersey, U.S.A. Cook Pottery Company, 1895. (l) LILLE, France. Hard paste. Stenciled and painted red. 1784.

a   b   c   d   e

(**a**) LILLE, France. Hard paste. Stenciled and painted red. 1784.
(**b-c**) NYON, Switzerland. Hard paste. Underglaze blue. 1780.
(**d**) SAVONA, Italy. Pescetto, potter. Fayence. 17th-18th century.
(**e**) NEWBURYPORT, Massachusetts, U.S.A. Merrimac Ceramic
Company. Est. 1897.

f   g

(**f**) NYON, Switzerland. Hard paste. Underglaze blue. 1780. (**g**)
SEVILLE, Spain. Glazed pottery. 19th century.

h   i   j   k   l   m

SECTION **ARROW**
See also Sections
T, Anchor, Lines

(**h**) LEEDS, Great Britain. Pottery. Impressed. Est. 1774. (**i**)
CAUGHLEY, Great Britain. Hard paste. Painted blue. 1754. (**j**)
BRISTOL, Great Britain. Pottery, porcelain. Painted blue, gold.
18th century. (**k**) GERMANY. Painted blue. 19th century (**l**)
BOW, Great Britain. Porcelain. 1750. (**m**) DERBY, Great Britain.
Porcelain. Circa 1830.

a   b   c   d   e   f

(**a**) DERBY, Great Britain. Porcelain. 1745-1848. (**b-c**) BOW, Great Britain. Porcelain. Est. 1750. (**d**) PLYMOUTH, Great Britain. Hard paste. Painted blue. 1768-1770. (**e-f**) BOW, Great Britain. Porcelain. Est. 1750.

g   h   i   j

(**g-h**) BOW, Great Britain. Soft paste. Painted blue. Est. 1750. (**i**) STOKE-ON-TRENT, Great Britain. Minton, factory. Hard paste. Painted gold, color. 1851. (**j**) LOWESTOFT, Great Britain. Robert Allen, painter. Porcelain. 1757-1780.

k   l   m   n   o

(**k**) YARMOUTH, Great Britain. W. Absolon, enameler. Porcelain, earthenware. Impressed. 19th century. (**l**) LEEDS, Great Britain. Pottery. Impressed. Est. 1774. (**m-n**) PARIS, France. Rue de la Roquette, factory. Hard paste. Painted blue. 1774. (**o**) PARIS, France. La Courtille, factory. Hard paste. Underglaze blue, incised. 1771.

a   b   c   d   e

(a) BOW, Great Britain. Soft paste. Painted blue. Est. 1750. (b) NYMPHENBURG, Germany. Impressed or incised. 18th century. (c-d) BOW, Great Britain. Soft paste. Painted blue. Est. 1750. (e) HOLLAND. Fayence. Delft. Painted blue. 1764.

f   g   h   i

(f-g) HOLLAND. De Drie Klokken (The Three Bells). Fayence. Delft. Est. 1671. (h-i) CAUGHLEY, Great Britain. Porcelain. Est. 1750.

j   k   l   m

(j) HANLEY, Great Britain. Impressed or printed. Circa 1870. (k) GIESSHUBEL, Germany. Porcelain, earthenware. Est. 1803. (l) EAST LIVERPOOL, Ohio, U.S.A. Harker Pottery Company. Printed. 1890. (m) DALE HALL, Great Britain. John and James Rogers, potters. Staffordshire. 1786-1842.

a   b   c   d

(a) PEORIA, Illinois, U.S.A. Peoria Pottery Company. 1873-1894.
(b) SHELTON, Great Britain. Job Ridgways, potter. Porcelain,
stone china. 1794-1802. (c-d) EAST LIVERPOOL, Ohio, U.S.A.
Harker Pottery Company. Printed. 1890.

SECTION **BIRD**
See also Sections
**Circle and Sign,
Crown and Circle,
Crown and Shield,
Shield, Square**

e   f   g   h   i   j

(e) BROOKLYN, New York, U.S.A. Union Porcelain Works. Est.
1874. (f) BROOKLYN, New York, U.S.A. Union Porcelain Works.
Est. 1874. (g) WHEELING, West Virginia, U.S.A. Wheeling Pottery Company. Est. 1879. (h-i-j) ANSBACH. Bavaria. Hard paste.
Painted blue. Est. 1706.

k   l   m   n   o

(k) ANSBACH, Bavaria. Hard paste. Est. 1706. (l) ST. PETERS-
BURG, Russia. Porcelain. Circa 1743. (m) CHARLOTTENBERG,
Germany. Porcelain. 1760. (n) ROYAL BERLIN, Germany. Est.
1751. (o) THE HAGUE, Holland. Fayence. 1775.

a   b   c   d   e

(**a**) THE HAGUE, Holland, Fayence. Painted blue. 1775. (**b**) THE HAGUE, Holland. Fayence. 1775. (**c**) THE HAGUE, Holland. Fayence. Painted blue. 1775. (**d**) LIVERPOOL, Great Britain. Herculaneum. Circa 1833. (**e**) FENTON, Great Britain. Hulme and Christie. 19th century.

f   g   h   i   j

(**f**) LIVERPOOL, Great Britain. Herculaneum. Circa 1833. (**g**) AMSTERDAM, Holland. Possibly at Arnheim. J. V. Kerckofi, artist. 1755-1770. (**h**) AMSTERDAM, Holland. Fayence. Circa 1780. (**i**) FLORENCE, Italy. Cantagalli. Fayence. Late 19th century. (**j**) BURSLEM, Great Britain. Charles Ford. 19th century.

k   l   m   n

(**k**) SOUTH AMBOY, New Jersey, U.S.A. Swan Hill Pottery. Hanks and Fish. 1849. (**l**) TUNSTALL, Great Britain. James Beech. Circa 1845. (**m**) TUNSTALL, Great Britain. Boulton, Machin, and Tennant. Late 19th century. (**n**) LIMOGES, France. 1842-1898.

a   b   c   d   e

(a) EAST LIVERPOOL, Ohio, U.S.A. Union Potteries Company. Late 19th century. (b)BOSTON, Massachusetts, U.S.A. New England Pottery Company. 1883-1886. (c) CROOKSVILLE, Ohio, U.S.A. Crooksville China Company. Late 19th century. (d) CORONA, New York, U.S.A. American Art Ceramic Company. Est. 1901. (e) EAST LIVERPOOL, Ohio, U.S.A. Homer Laughlin China Company. Est. 1773.

f   g   h   i

(f) EAST LIVERPOOL, Ohio, U.S.A. Potters Cooperative Company. Circa 1880. (g) TRENTON, New Jersey, U.S.A. Glasgow Pottery Company. John Moses and Sons. 1863-1890. (h) SEVRES, France. 1852 (i) SEVRES, France. Hard paste. Painted red. Circa 1810.

j   k   l   m   n

(j) LIVERPOOL, Ohio, U.S.A. John E. Goodwin. Printed. Stoneware. 1844-1853. (k) NEW YORK, New York, U.S.A. East Morrisania China Works. Late 19th century. (l) NEW MILFORD, Connecticut, U.S.A. New Milford Pottery Company. Est. 1886. (m) EAST LIVERPOOL, Ohio, U.S.A. Knowles, Taylor, and Knowles. Est. 1870. (n) STOKE-ON-TRENT, Great Britain. W. H. Goss. Late 19th century.

a   b   c   d

(a) EAST LIVERPOOL, Ohio, U.S.A. Vodrey Brothers. 1857-1885.
(b) TRENTON, New Jersey, U.S.A. American Crockery Company.
Est. 1876. (c) STOKE-ON-TRENT, Great Britain. T. Mayer. Circa
1829. (d) CINCINNATI, Ohio, U.S.A. Rookwood Potteries. Est.
1879.

Section **BOWL
AND URN**

e   f   g   h   i

(e-f) HOLLAND. De Porcelyn Fles (The Porcelain Bottle). Fayence. Delft. 1770. (g) HOLLAND. Thoovt and Labouchere. Fayence. Delft. 1895. (h) ALT-ROHLAU, Germany. Pottery, porcelain. Est. 1813. (i) GERMANY. Schemlzer and Gericke. Est. 1865.

j   k   l   m

(j) LIMOGES, France. Porcelain. Circa 1875. (k-l) WEDG-
WOOD, Great Britain. Porcelain. Printed black, color. After 1878.
(m) BEAVER FALLS, Pennsylvania, U.S.A. Mayer Pottery Company. Est. 1880.

a   **b**   **c**   **d**

(a) BRISTOL, Great Britain. Hard paste. Printed blue. 1800. (b) JERSEY CITY, New Jersey, U.S.A. American Pottery Manufacturing Company. 1833-1840. (c) SHELTON, Great Britain. Job Ridgways, potter. 1794. (d) GREAT BRITAIN. Podmore, Walker, and Company. Circa 1755.

SECTION **CIRCLE AND SIGN**
See also Sections **O, Crown and Circle, Shield**

   e   f   g   h   i

(e) FAENZA, Italy. Fayence. 16th century. (f) COPENHAGEN, Denmark. Fayence. Iron porcelain. 1929. (g) STOKE-ON-TRENT, Great Britain. Spode, factory. Impressed. 1784. (h) FAENZA, Italy. Fayence. 16th century. (i) HOCHST, Germany. Hard paste. Painted blue, red, gold. 1750-1765.

   j   **k**   **l**   **m**   **n**

(j) TYLERSPORT, Pennsylvania, U.S.A. Michael School (Scholl). Impressed. Circa 1830. (k-l) FAENZA, Italy. Fayence. 16th century. (m-n) VALENCIA, Spain. Fayence. 16th century.

a   b   c   d   e

(**a-b**) WORCESTER, Great Britain. Hard paste. Underglaze blue.
Est. 1751. (**c-d-e**) FAENZA, Italy. Fayence. 16th century.

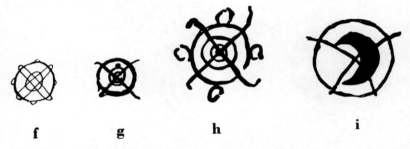

f   g   h   i

(**f-g-h-i**) FAENZA, Italy. Fayence. 16th century.

j   k   l   m   n

(**j**) BOW, Great Britain. Soft paste. Est. 1750. (**k**) HOCHST, Ger-
many. Porcelain, fayence. Painted gold, color. Est. 1746. (**l**) WOR-
CESTER, Great Britain. Kerr and Binns. Porcelain. 1852-1862. (**m**)
SEGOVIA, Spain. 19th century. (**n**) SARREGUEMINES, France.
Fayence, porcelain. Est. 1770.

a   b   c   d   e

(a) HOLLAND, De Romeyn (The Roman). Fayence. Delft. 1675.
(b) WOODBRIDGE, New Jersey, U.S.A. C. and H. Poillon. 19th
century. (c) TRENTON, New Jersey, U.S.A. Ott and Brewer. Circa
1875. (d) PEORIA, Illinois, U.S.A. Peoria Pottery Company. Circa
1885. (e) NEW YORK CITY, New York, U.S.A. Carr and Morrison.
Circa 1875.

f   g   h   i   j

(f) GERMANY. Porcelain. Circa 1855. (g-h) HOCHST, Germany.
Fayence, hard paste. Painted blue, red, gold. 1750-1765. (i) SHEL-
TON, Great Britain. Joshua Heath, potter. Circa 1760. (j)
HOCHST, Germany. Fayence, hard paste. Painted blue, red, gold.
1750.

k   l   m   n   o

(k) HOLLAND, De Fortuyn (The Fortune). Fayence. Delft.
Painted blue. 1691. (l) CHELSEA, Massachusetts, U.S.A. Low Art
Tile Company. Est. 1888. (m) WHEELING, West Virginia, U.S.A.
Wheeling Pottery Company. Est. 1879. (n) HOLLAND. Fayence.
Delft. Painted blue. 1680. (o) JERSEY CITY, New Jersey, U.S.A.
Jersey City Pottery Company. Est. 1840.

a   b   c   d   e

(a) JERSEY CITY, New Jersey, U.S.A. American Pottery Company. Est. 1840. (b-c) TRENTON, New Jersey, U.S.A. Anchor Pottery Company. Printed. After 1894. (d) KITTANNING, Pennsylvania, U.S.A. Wick China Company. 19th century. (e) BALTIMORE, Maryland, U.S.A. Haynes, Bennett, and Company. After 1890.

f   g   h   i   j

(f) MINTON, England. Hard paste. After 1868. (g) ETRURIA, Great Britain. Wedgwood and Bentley, factory. 1769-1780. (h) LUXEMBOURG, Belgium. Fayence. Est. 1767. (i) TRENTON, New Jersey, U.S.A. Burgess and Campbell. Impressed. Est. 1879. (j) GIESSHUBEL, Germany. Porcelain, fayence. Circa 1850.

k   l   m   n

(k) LIMOGES, France. Charles Field Haviland Company. 1882. (l) CHOISY-LE-ROY, France. Hard Paste. Est. 1785. (m) DERBY, Great Britain. Porcelain. Est. 1745-1848. (n) TRENTON, New Jersey, U.S.A. Trenton Potteries Company. Est. 1865.

a   b   c   d   e

(a) SEVRES, France. Overglaze red. Year of decoration. 1872-1899.
(b) MONTPELLIER, France. Pottery. Impressed. 1800. (c)
SEVRES, France. Red. Year of gilding. 1872-1899. (d) TRENTON,
New Jersey, U.S.A. Cook Pottery Company. 1894-1900. (e) BALTI-
MORE, Maryland, U.S.A. D. F. Haynes and Company. Est. 1879.

f   g   h   i

(f) WOODBRIDGE, New Jersey, U.S.A. Salamander Works. Im-
pressed. 1825-1900. (g-h) JERSEY CITY, New Jersey, U.S.A. Jersey
City Pottery Company. 1829-1833. (i) LAMBETH, Great Britain.
Doulton Company. After 1891.

j   k   l   m

(j) TRENTON, New Jersey, U.S.A. Cook Pottery Company. Circa
1900. (k) PHOENIXVILLE, Pennsylvania, U.S.A. Griffen, Smith,
and Hill. Impressed. Circa 1880. (l) BURSLEM, Great Britain.
Enoch Wood and Sons. 1790. (m) ILMENAU, Germany. Porcelain. 19th century.

a   b   c   d

(a) PARIS, France. Porcelain. 1857. (b) GERMANY. Benedikt Brothers. 1884. (c) BURSLEM, Great Britain. E. F. Bodley and Company. Earthenware. After 1860. (d) TRENTON, New Jersey, U.S.A. Glasgow Pottery Company. Circa 1875.

e   f   g   h   i

(e) LIVERPOOL, Ohio, U.S.A. John Goodwin. Stoneware. Printed. Est. 1844. (f) GOTHA, Germany. Porcelain. Est. 1757. (g) ALT-ROHLAU, Germany. Cream-colored earthenware. Est. 1813. (h) TRENTON, New Jersey, U.S.A. Glasgow Pottery Company. 1863-1890. (i) KEENE, New Hampshire, U.S.A. Hampshire Pottery Company. Est. 1871.

j   k   l   m   n

(j) EAST LIVERPOOL, Ohio, U.S.A. Harker Pottery Company. Circa 1840. (k) HAVILAND, France. Porcelain. Green, brown, tan. About 1885. (l-m) HAVILAND, France. Whiteware. Painted green, reddish brown. Circa 1876. (n) JERSEY CITY, New Jersey, U.S.A. D. J. Henderson. Impressed. Circa 1830.

a   b   c   d

(a) LETTIN, Germany. Est. 1858. (b) EAST LIVERPOOL, Ohio, U.S.A. Homer Laughlin China Company. Printed. Est. 1873. (c) HANLEY, Great Britain. Humphrey Palmer. Staffordshire. Circa 1760. (d) WHEELING, West Virginia, U.S.A. Wheeling Pottery Company. Est. 1879.

e   f   g   h   i

(e) WELLSVILLE, Ohio, U.S.A. Wellsville China Company. Est. 1879. (f) HANLEY, Great Britain. I. Neale. 1786. (g) PHOENIX-VILLE, Pennsylvania, U.S.A. Beerbower and Griffen. Est. 1877. (h) BALTIMORE, Maryland, U.S.A. Edwin Bennett. (Mark often seen without circle.) 1856-1890. (i) POUGHKEEPSIE, New York, U.S.A. Jacob Caire. Impressed. Circa 1850.

j   k   l   m   n

(j) WOOSTER, Ohio, U.S.A. Joseph Routson. Late 19th century. (k) BUEN RETIRO, Spain. Hard paste. 1805. (l) BERLIN, Germany. Soft paste. Painted blue. 1850. (m) LAMBETH, Great Britain. Doulton. Pottery. 1872. (n) SEVRES, France. Painted red. Circa 1890.

a b   c   d   e

(a-b-c) LIMOGES, France. Hard paste. 1842-1898. (d) DERBY,
Great Britain. William Locker, owner. Porcelain. 1848. (e) FLOR-
SHEIM, Germany. Fayence. Est. 1773.

f   g   h   i   j

(f) SEVRES, France. Decorator's mark. Painted red. After 1940.
(g) BALTIMORE, Maryland, U.S.A. D. F. Haynes and Company.
Est. 1879. (h) STOKE-ON-TRENT, Great Britain. Minton, factory.
1870. (i) MONTPELLIER, France. Fayence. 1834. (j) SEVRES,
France. Soft paste, hard paste. 1890.

k   l   m   n   o

(k) NEW CASTLE, Pennsylvania, U.S.A. New Castle Pottery Company. 19th century. (l) SHELTON, Great Britain. Fayence. Printed
color. 1820. (m) ORLEANS, France. Hard paste. Circa 1800. (n)
EAST LIVERPOOL, Ohio, U.S.A. Vodrey Brothers. Circa 1875.
(o) DOCCIA, Italy. 18th-19th century.

a   b   c   d   e

(a) WELLSVILLE, Ohio, U.S.A. Wellsville China Company. Est. 1879. (b) TRENTON. New Jersey, U.S.A. Glasgow Pottery Company. Circa 1875. (c) TRENTON, New Jersey, U.S.A. American Art China Works. Est. 1891. (d) CINCINNATI, Ohio, U.S.A. Cincinnati Art Pottery Company. Est. 1879. (e) SEVRES, France. Hard paste. Painted red. 1850.

f   g   h   i   j

(f) URBINO, Italy. Pottery. 16th century. (g) BUEN RETIRO, Spain. Hard paste. Circa 1805. (h) ZANESVILLE, Ohio, U.S.A. Roseville Pottery Company. 19th century. (i) ST. AMAND LES EAUX, France. Soft paste. 1800. (j) SWINTON, Great Britain. Don Pottery. Impressed or printed blue. 19th century.

k   l   m   n   o

(k) GERMANY. Hornberg. Fayence. Late 19th century. (l) MOABIT, Germany. 1835. (m-n) SEVRES, France. Hard paste. Printed gold, blue, color. 1830-1848. (o) NEW CASTLE, Pennsylvania, U.S.A. Shenango China Company. 19th century.

a   b   c   d   e

(a) EAST LIVERPOOL. Ohio, U.S.A. Smith-Phillips China· Company. Late 19th century. (b) LONGPORT, Great Britain. Stubbs and Kent. Circa 1805. (c) GERMANY. Fayence. 19th century. (d) Syracuse, New York, U.S.A. Onandaga Pottery Company. Est. 1871. (e) TILLOWITZ, Germany. Fayence, earthenware. Est. 1804.

f   g   h   i   j

(f) STOKE-ON-TRENT, Great Britain. T. Mayer. Circa 1830. (g) CHURCH GRESLEY, Great Britain. Porcelain. 1794-1800. (h) BEAVER FALLS, Pennsylvania, U.S.A. Mayer Pottery Company. Est. 1881. (i) BROOKLYN, New York, U.S.A. Union Porcelain Works. Est. 1875. (j) TRENTON, New Jersey, U.S.A. Crescent Pottery Company. Est. 1881.

k   l   m   n   o

(k) TILTONVILLE, Ohio, U.S.A. Vance Faience Company. Impressed. After 1880. (l) COLORADO SPRINGS, Colorado, U.S.A. Van Briggle Pottery Company. Est. 1901. (m) BALTIMORE, Maryland, U.S.A. Edwin Bennett. Circa 1875. (n) ETRURIA, Great Britain. Wedgwood and Bentley. Pottery and hard paste. Impressed. 1769-1780. (o) PEORIA, Illinois. Peoria Pottery Company. 1873-1894.

a   b   c   d

(a) TUNSTALL, Great Britain. Blue printed ware. 1804-1840. (b) HULL, Great Britain. Bellevue Pottery Company. 1825. (c) METT-LACH, Germany. Villeroy and Boch. 19th-20th century. (d) STOKE-ON-TRENT, Great Britain. W. T. Copeland and Sons. Hard paste, fayence. 1833-1847.

e   f   g   h

(e-f) STOKE-ON-TRENT, Great Britain. Copeland and Garrett. 1833-1847. (g) GERMANY. F. A. Mehlem, factory. Est. 1836. (h) TRENTON, New Jersey, U.S.A. Glasgow Pottery Company. Circa 1875.

i   j   k   l   m

(i) LIVERPOOL, Ohio, U.S.A. Knowles, Taylor, and Knowles. After 1870. (j) LIMOGES, France. J. Pouyat, potter. Earthenware. 1842. (k) METTLACH, Germany. Fayence. Glazed earthenware. Est. 1809. (l) MOUSTIERS, France. Fayence. Stenciled. 1780. (m) WELLSVILLE, Ohio, U.S.A. Wellsville China Company. Est. 1879.

a   b   c   d   e

(a) TRENTON, New Jersey, U.S.A. Ott and Brewer. 1867-1892.
(b) METTLACH, Germany. Villeroy and Boch. 19th-20th century.
(c) TRENTON, New Jersey, U.S.A. Burgess and Campbell. Est.
1879. (d) EAST LIVERPOOL, Ohio, U.S.A. Burford Brothers Pottery Company. 1875-1900. (e) LIVERPOOL, Ohio, U.S.A. John
Goodwin. Printed. Est. 1844.

f   g   h   i   j

(f-g-h-i-j) FORD CITY, Pennsylvania, U.S.A. Ford City Company,
Earthenware. Late 19th century.

k   l   m   n   o

(k) TRENTON, New Jersey, U.S.A. Burroughs and Mountford.
Circa 1880. (l) TRENTON, New Jersey, U.S.A. Glasgow Pottery
Company. Circa 1875. (m) BEAVER FALLS, Pennsylvania, U.S.A.
Mayer Pottery Company. Est. 1881. (n-o) TRENTON, New Jersey,
U.S.A. Burgess and Campbell. Est. 1879.

a   b   c   d   e

(**a-b**) TRENTON, New Jersey, U.S.A. Burgess and Campbell. Est. 1879. (**c**) EAST LIVERPOOL, Ohio, U.S.A. Knowles, Taylor, and Knowles. Circa 1870. (**d**) TRENTON, New Jersey, U.S.A. Glasgow Pottery Company. Circa 1875. (**e**) BEAVER FALLS, Pennsylvania, U.S.A. Mayer Pottery Company. Est. 1881.

f   g   h   i   j

(**f**) BEAVER FALLS, Pennsylvania, U.S.A. Mayer Pottery Company. Est. 1881. (**g**) HANLEY, Great Britain. Late 19th century. (**h-i**) TRENTON, New Jersey, U.S.A. Anchor Pottery Company. Printed. 1894. (**j**) TRENTON, New Jersey, U.S.A. Ceramic Art Company. Lenox. Hard paste. Painted violet, 1894-1896; green or gold, 1897-1898; black, 1898-1906.

k   l   m   n

(**k**) EAST LIVERPOOL, Ohio, U.S.A. Homer Laughlin China Company. Printed. Est. 1872. (**l-m**) ESTE, Italy. Porcelain. 18th-19th century. (**n**) STOKE-ON-TRENT, Great Britain. E. Brain and Company Ltd. Foley China. 20th century.

ALTE FABRIKMARKE

a   b   c   d

(a) TRENTON, New Jersey, U.S.A. Greenwood Pottery. Printed.
Est. 1864. (b) GERMANY. Hutschenreuther. Hard paste. 1906.
(c) TRENTON, New Jersey, U.S.A. Maddock Pottery Company.
After 1893. (d) STOKE-ON-TRENT, Great Britain. Grimwade
Brothers. After 1891.

e   f   g   h   i

(e) ELIZABETH, New Jersey, U.S.A. L. B. Beerbower (Beer-
bauer) and Company. Impressed. After 1879. (f) EAST LIVER-
POOL, Ohio, U.S.A. Knowles, Taylor, and Knowles. After 1870.
(g) TRENTON, .New Jersey, U.S.A. Crescent Pottery Company.
Est. 1881. (h) STOCKTON, California, U.S.A. Stockton Art Pottery
Company. 19th century. (i) JERSEY CITY, New Jersey, U.S.A.
American Pottery Company. Impressed, printed. 1833-1845.

j   k   l   m

(j) ANDENNE, Belgium. Bernard Lammens, owner, 1820. (k-l)
SEVRES, France. Hard paste. Printed color. Pieces made for roy-
alty. Circa 1834. (m) GERMANY. Schmidt Brothers. Est. 1847.

a   b   c   d

(a) EAST LIVERPOOL, Ohio, U.S.A. C. C. Thompson Pottery
Company. Est. 1888. (b) TRENTON, New Jersey, U.S.A. Ott and
Brewer (Otter and Brewer) Circa 1875. (c) RHEINSBERG, Ger-
many. Fayence. Est. 1762. (d) TRENTON, New Jersey, U.S.A.
Mercer Pottery Company. White earthenware. Est. 1868.

e   f   g   h   i

(e) COLOGNE, Germany. Pottery. 17th century. (f.) TUNSTALL,
Great Britain. Alfred Meakin. Est. 1881. (g) TRENTON, New Jer-
sey, U.S.A. Burroughs and Mountford. Circa 1880. (h) WOR-
CESTER, Great Britain. Edward Locke and Company. After 1891.
(i) STOKE-ON-TRENT, Great Britain. Minton, factory. Hard paste.
After 1868.

j   k   l   m   n

(j) BALTIMORE, Maryland, U.S.A. Edwin Bennett. Circa 1875.
(k) LONGTON, Great Britain. J. Holdcraft. 19th century. (l)
EAST LIVERPOOL, Ohio, U.S.A. Brunt, Bloor, and Martin. After
1875. (m) EAST LIVERPOOL, Ohio, U.S.A. Globe Pottery Company. Est. 1888. (n) TRENTON, New Jersey, U.S.A. Ott and
Brewer. Circa 1875.

a   b   c   d

(a) TRENTON, New Jersey, U.S.A. Mercer Pottery Company. Est. 1868. (b-c) BALTIMORE, Maryland, U.S.A. Circa 1875. (d) CHITTENANGO, New York, U.S.A. Chittenango Pottery Company. Est. 1897.

e   f   g   h   i

(e) WHEELING, West Virginia, U.S.A. Wheeling Pottery Company. Est. 1879. (f-g) TRENTON, New Jersey, U.S.A. Willetts Manufacturing Company. Circa 1860. (h) EAST LIVERPOOL, Ohio, U.S.A. Burford Brothers Pottery Company. Circa 1885. (i) STOKE-ON-TRENT, Great Britain. Minton, factory. After 1870.

j   k   l   m

(j) LONGTON, Great Britain. Moore Brothers. Late 19th century. (k) STOKE-ON-TRENT, Great Britain. Minton, factory. 19th-20th century. (l) TRENTON, New Jersey, U.S.A. Crescent Pottery Company. Est. 1881. (m) LONGTON, Great Britain. 20th century.

a   b   c   d   e

(**a-b**) COBRIDGE, Great Britain. Brownfield Company. After 1891.
(**c**) TRENTON, New Jersey, U.S.A. Anchor Pottery Company.
Printed. After 1891. (**d**) EAST LIVERPOOL, Ohio, U.S.A. Brunt,
Bloor, and Martin. 1875. (**e**) TRENTON, New Jersey, U.S.A. Empire Pottery Company. Circa 1875.

f   g   h   i   j

(**f**) LIMOGES, France. Charles Field Haviland. 1900-1941. (**g**)
EAST LIVERPOOL, Ohio, U.S.A. Vodrey Brothers, Circa 1875.
(**h-i**) STEUBENVILLE, Ohio, U.S.A. Steubenville Pottery Company. Est. 1887. (**j**) TRENTON, New Jersey, U:S.A. Lenox China
Company. Hard paste. 1906-1952.

k   l   m   n

(**k**) TRENTON, New Jersey, U.S.A. Lenox China Company. Hard
paste. Decorated ware. Printed violet, 1894-1896; green or gold,
1897-1906. (**l**) WELLSVILLE, Ohio, U.S.A. Circa 1880. (**m**)
TRENTON, New Jersey. U.S.A. Glasgow Pottery Company. Circa
1875. (**n**) STOKE-ON-TRENT, Great Britain. W. T. Copeland and
Sons. Spode. 1847-1891.

a   b   c   d   e

(**a**) WHEELING, West Virginia, U.S.A. Wheeling Pottery Company. Est. 1879. (**b-c**) TRENTON, New Jersey, U.S.A. Ceramic Art Company. Lenox. After 1891. (**d**) EAST LIVERPOOL, Ohio, U.S.A. Union Potteries Company. 19th century. (**e**) TRENTON, New Jersey, U.S.A. Keystone Pottery Company. 19th century.

f   g   h   i

(**f-g**) TEINITZ, Germany. Impressed or stamped. 1801-1839. (**h**) WHEELING, West Virginia, U.S.A. Wheeling Pottery Company. Est. 1879. (**i**) ALT-ROHLAU, Germany, 1813.

j   k

(**j**) SHELTON, Great Britain. Job Ridgway, potter. Stone china. 1802. (**k**) LANE DELPH, Great Britain. Staffordshire. Circa 1800.

a   b   c

(**a**) STOKE-ON-TRENT, Great Britain. Copeland and Garrett. Spode. 1833-1847. (**b**) STOKE-ON-TRENT, Great Britain. Minton factory. Hard paste. Printed 1800. (**c**) SHARTLESVILLE, Pennsylvania, U.S.A. J. S. Henne. Impressed. 1800.

d   e   f

(**d-e**) SCHLAGGENWALD, Germany. 1793-1866. (**f**) METTLACH, Germany. Villeroy and Boch. 1842.

g   h   i   j

(**g**) TRENTON, New Jersey, U.S.A. Millington, Astbury, and Poulson. 1859-1870. (**h**) CREIL, France. Fayence. 1794-1895. (**i**) BENNINGTON, Vermont, U.S.A. United States Pottery. Impressed. Circa 1855. (**j**) COPENHAGEN, Denmark. Fayence. Stamped. 1863.

a   b   c   d

(**a**) JERSEY CITY, New Jersey, U.S.A. American Pottery Manufacturing Company. Underglaze, printed. Circa 1835. (**b**) HOLLAND. Arij de Milde, artist. Redware. 1680-1708. (**c**) BURTON-ON-TRENT, Great Britain. Ashby Potter's Guild. Pottery. Est. 1909. (**d**) GERMANY. Gebr. Bauscher. Restaurant china. 1881-1927.

e   f   g   h   i

(**e**) ANDENNE, Belgium. B. Lammens, owner. Fayence. Impressed. 1820. (**f**) DERBY, Great Britain. Porcelain. 1811-1848. (**g**) SWINTON, Great Britain. Bramels and Company. Rockingham Works. 1840. (**h**) CINCINNATI, Ohio, U.S.A. Cincinnati Art Pottery Company. Est. 1879. (**i**) GERMANY. Fischern. Porcelain. 1848.

j   k   l   m

(**j**) EAST LIVERPOOL, Ohio, U.S.A. Cartwright Brothers. 1890. (**k**) CHOISY-LE-ROY, France. Hard paste. 1804. (**l**) BALTIMORE, Maryland, U.S.A. F. Haynes and Company. 1880. (**m**) STOKE-ON-TRENT, Great Britain. Spode, factory. 20th century.

a   b   c   d   e

(a) TRENTON, New Jersey, U.S.A. Delaware Pottery Company. Est. 1884. (b) SWANSEA, Great Britain. Circa 1865. (c) LAMBETH, Great Britain. Doulton, factory.1840. (d) READING, Pennsylvania, U.S.A. Daniel Shenfelder. Impressed. Est. 1869. (e) MONTET, France. Pottery. Impressed. 1800.

f   g   h   i

(f) ALCORA, Spain. Porcelain. Painted red, gold, black. 1727-1749. (g) UZES, France. Pottery. Impressed. 1800. (h) JERSEY CITY, New Jersey, U.S.A. D. and J. Henderson. Impressed. 1829-1833. (i) HOLLAND. H. v. Middledyk. Fayence. Delft. 1764.

j   k   l

(j) EAST LIVERPOOL, Ohio, U.S.A. Vodrey Brothers. Circa 1875. (k) TROY, New York, U.S.A. J. Chapman. 1815. (l) SCOTLAND. J. and M. P. Bell. After 1842.

a   b   c   d   e

(a) BENNINGTON, Vermont, U.S.A. Lyman Fenton Company. 1849. (b) TRENTON, New Jersey, U.S.A. Millington, Astbury, and Poulson. 1859-1870. (c-d) SEVRES, France. Painted black, hard paste; painted blue on soft paste. 1917-1920. (e) VAL-SOUS-MEUDON, France. Mittenhoff and Mouron, owners. White earthenware. 1806.

f   g   h   i   j

(f) NEW YORK, New York, U.S.A. Morrison and Carr. Circa 1870. (g) BOSTON, Massachusetts. New England Pottery Company. 1888. (h) GERMANY. Nordd Steingut Fabrik. Est. 1870. (i) CINCINNATI, Ohio, U.S.A. Rookwood Pottery Company. Est. 1876. (j) SEVRES, France. Painted black on hard paste; blue on soft paste. 1912-1917, 1921-1927.

k   l   m   n   o

(k) SEVRES, France. Issued without decoration. 1871. (l) WOODBRIDGE, New York, U.S.A. Salamander Works. Impressed. 1848. (m) BALTIMORE, Maryland, U.S.A. F. Haynes and Company. Est. 1882. (n) BOHEMIA. Schelten. Porcelain. 1855. (o) TRENTON, New Jersey, U.S.A. Thomas Maddock's Sons Company. 1902.

a   b   c   d   e   f

(a) LEEDS, Great Britain. Thomas Nicholson and Company. After 1854. (b) TRENTON, New Jersey, U.S.A. Delaware Pottery Company. Est. 1884. (c) BENNINGTON, Vermont, U.S.A. United States Pottery Company. 1852-1858. (d-e) BEAVER FALLS, Pennsylvania, U.S.A. Mayer Pottery Company. Est. 1881. (f) ALT-ROHLAU, Germany. 1813.

g   h   i   j   k   l

(g) COLOGNE, Germany. Pottery. Painted blue.. 17th century. (h) EAST LIVERPOOL, Ohio, U.S.A. Taylor, Smith, and Taylor Company. Est. 1899. (i) FLORENCE, Italy. Soft paste. Painted color. 16th century. (j) LIMBACH, Germany. Hard paste. Painted 1761. (k) TURKEY. 17th or 18th century. (l) BOURG-LA-REINE, France. Hard paste. Painted 1773.

SECTION **COPIES OF ORIENTAL MARKS** See also Section **Lines**

m   n   o   p   q

(m) ELBOGEN, Bohemia. Hard paste. Impressed. 1810. (n) CAUGHLEY, Great Britain. 1772-1799. (o) CAUGHLEY, Great Britain. 1772-1799. (p) OFFENBACH, Germany. Lay, artist. Fayence. 1739. (q) WORCESTER, Great Britain. Before 1783.

a   b   c   d   e

(a) WORCESTER, Great Britain. Before 1783. (b) WORCESTER, Great Britain. 1751-1783. (c) WORCESTER, Great Britain. Painted red, blue. Circa 1780. (d) WORCESTER, Great Britain. 1751-1781. (e) WORCESTER, Great Britain. Dr. Wall. 1751-1783.

f   g   h   i   j

(f) HOLLAND. Fayence. Delft. Painted blue. Circa 1800. (g) HOLLAND. Fayence. Delft. Painted blue. Circa 1800. (h) HOLLAND. De Romeyn (The Roman). Fayence. Delft. 1671. (i) WORCESTER, Great Britain. 1751-1783. (j) WORCESTER, Great Britain. Dr. Wall. Porcelain. 1751-1783.

k   l   m   n   o

(k) WORCESTER, Great Britain. Painted blue. 1751. (l) BURSLEM. Great Britain. John and David Elers. 1688-1710. (m) MEISSEN, Germany. Hard paste, Bottger ware. Painted blue. Circa 1700. (n-o) MEISSEN, Germany. Bottger red ware. Circa 1700.

a   b   c   d

(**a-b**) MEISSEN, Germany. Bottger red ware: Circa 1700. (**c**) COALBROOKDALE, Great Britain. Hard paste. 1796-1861. (**d**) PARIS, France. Samson, the imitator. Mark on imitation Lowestoft. Circa 1875.

SECTION
CRESCENT
See also Sections
C, G, Lines

e   f   g   h   i   j

(**e**) BOW, Great Britain. 1750-1775. (**f-g**) CAUGHLEY, Great Britain. Painted blue. 1750-1814. (**h-i**) WORCESTER, Great Britain. Hard paste. 1751-1800. (**j**) CAUGHLEY, Great Britain. 1750-1814.

k   l   m   n   o   p

(**k**) WORCESTER, Great Britain. Hard paste. 1751-1800. (**l**) BOW, Great Britain. Porcelain. 1750-1775. (**m**) CAUGHLEY, Great Britain. 1750-1814. (**n**) WORCESTER, Great Britain. Painted color. 1751-1800. (**o**) PINXTON, Great Britain. Soft paste. 1796-1801. (**p**) NYMPHENBERG, Germany. Porcelain. Impressed or incised. 18th century.

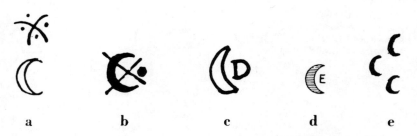

a b c d e

(**a**) TURKEY. Porcelain. Circa 1850. (**b**) FAENZA, Italy. Fayence. 16th century. (**c**) CAUGHLEY, Great Britain. 1750-1814. (**d**) WORCESTER, Great Britain. Blueware. 1751-1800. (**e**) MUNDEN, Germany. Fayence. 18th century.

f g h i j k

(**f-g-h**) MARIEBERG, Sweden. Pottery and soft paste. Painted color. 1750. (**i**) WORCESTER, Great Britain. Flight. Hard paste. Painted blue. 1783-1792. (**j**) CAUGHLEY, Great Britain. Hard paste. Painted blue. 1750. (**k**) EAST LIVERPOOL, Ohio, U.S.A. William Brunt Pottery Company. 1850-1895.

l m n o p

(**l-m**) TRENTON, New Jersey, U.S.A. Ott (Otter) and Brewer. 1876. (**n-o**) STOKE-ON-TRENT, Great Britain. 19th-20th century. (**p**) BEAVER FALLS, Pennsylvania, U.S.A. Mayer Pottery Company. Est. 1881.

a   b   c   d   e

(a) NOTTINGHAM, Great Britain. Lovatt and Lovatt. 19th-20th
century. (b) EDGERTON, Wisconsin, U.S.A. Pauline Pottery Company. Impressed. 1888. (c-d) DERBY, Great Britain. 1755-1770.
(e) EDGERTON, Wisconsin, U.S.A. Pauline Pottery Company.
Impressed. Est. 1883.

f   g   h   i   j

(f) TURIN, Italy. Fayence. 16th-17th century. (g) EVANSVILLE,
Indiana, U.S.A. Crown Pottery Company. Est. 1891. (h) LONG-
TON, Great Britain. R. H. Plant and Company. 19th century.
(i) BUEN RETIRO, Spain. Soft paste. 1759-1808. (j) LUDWIGS-
BURG, Germany. Hard paste. Painted blue. 1758-1793.

k   l   m   n   o   p

(k) LUDWIGSBURG, Germany. Hard paste. Painted blue. 1758-
1793; or BUEN RETIRO, Spain. Soft paste and pottery. Painted
color. 1760. (l) NIDERVILLER, France. Fayence, porcelain.
Painted blue. Est. 1754. (m) SAINT PETERSBURG, Russia. Fayence, porcelain. Painted color. 1796-1801. (n) DERBY, Great Britain. Soft paste. Painted gold. 1770-1810. (o) CHELSEA, Great
Britain. Underglaze blue. 1745-1784. (p) SAINT PETERSBURG,
Russia. Hard paste. Painted color. 1801.

a   b   c   d   e

(**a**) SAINT PETERSBURG, Russia. Hard paste. Painted blue or color. 1855-1881. (**b**) PARIS, France. Hard paste. Painted red. 1778. (**c**) SAINT PETERSBURG, Russia. 1855-1881. (**d**) SAINT PE-TERSBURG, Russia. One dot added for each year after 1870. (This is really four marks.) 1871-1881. (**e**) NAPLES, Italy. 18th century.

f   g   h   i   j

(**f**) SAVONA, Italy. 17th-18th century. (**g-h-i**) PARIS, France. Rue Thiroux, factory. 1775-1869. (**j**) PARIS, France. Hard paste. Painted red. 18th century.

k   l   m   n   o

(**k**) VENICE, Italy. 1753. (**l**) MEISSEN, Germany. Bottger red ware. 18th century. (**m**) BRUSSELS, Belgium. Hard paste. Painted color. 1800. (**n**) DERBY, Great Britain. Bloor. 1811-1848. (**o**) NAPLES, Italy. 18th century.

a   b   c   d   e

(a) NAPLES, Italy. 17th century. (b) WORCESTER, Great Britain. Hard paste. 1813-1840. (c) NAPLES, Italy. 17th century. (d) FRIEDBURG, Germany. Fayence. 1768. (e) SEVRES, France. 1830-1848.

f   g   h   i   j

(f) PARIS, France. Hard paste. Painted blue. 1769. (g) BRUSSELS, Belgium. 19th century. (h) SEVRES, France. Hard paste. Painted blue. 1829. (i-j) DERBY, Great Britain. Porcelain. Painted red, violet. 1780.

k   l   m   n   o

(k) CLIGNANCOURT, France. Est. 1771. (l) MEISSEN, Germany. After 1880. (m) DERBY, Great Britain. Bloor. 1811-1848. (n) HILDESHEIM, Germany. Hard paste. Painted blue. 1760. (o) FULDA, Germany. Hard paste. Painted blue. 1763-1780.

a   b   c   d   e

(**a**) GINORI, Italy. Capo-di-Monte, factory. Soft paste. Painted color. 1780. (**b**) LEEDS, Great Britain. Earthenware. Est. 1760. (**c-d-e**) SAINT PETERSBURG, Russia. Porcelain. Painted color. Est. 1744.

f   g   h   i   j

(**f**) GERMANY. Hesse Darmstadt. Hard paste. Painted blue. 1756. (**g-h-i-j**) VINCENNES, France. Hard paste. 1765.

k   l   m   n   o

(**k**) VINCENNES, France. Hard paste. 1765. (**l-m**) CLIGNAN-COURT, France. Painted red. Est. 1771. (**n**) BUEN RETIRO, Spain. Soft paste. 1759-1808. (**o**) NAPLES, Italy. 17th century.

a   b   c   d   e

(**a-b**) BUEN RETIRO, Spain. Hard paste, soft paste. 1759-1808.
(**c-d-e**) GINORI, Italy. Capo-di-Monte, factory. Soft paste. Painted
red, blue, or impressed: 18th century.

f   g   h   i   j

(**f-g**) GINORI, Italy. Capo-di-Monte, factory. Circa 1820. (**h**) OR-
LEANS, France. Pottery. Painted color. 1753. (**i**) LUDWIGSBURG,
Germany. Porcelain, fayence. 1756-1824. (**j**) GINORI, Italy. Painted
red, color. Circa 1773.

k   l   m   n   o

(**k**) GINORI, Italy. Capo-di-Monte, factory. Painted red, color.
Circa 1773. (**l**) SEVRES, France. Hard paste, soft paste. Painted
color. 1854. (**m**) MEISSEN, Germany. Sachsiche Porzellen Manufactur. Hard paste. Painted blue. 1750. (**n**) SAVONA, Italy. 17th-
18th century. (**o**) SEVRES, France. 1830-1848.

a   b   c   d   e

(a) SEVRES, France. Hard paste. Impressed or printed color. 1845.
(b) FRANKENTHAL, Germany. Hard paste. Painted blue. 1761.
(c) LUDWIGSBURG, Germany. Hard paste. Painted blue. 1806.
(d) VISTA ALEGRE, Portugal. Porcelain. Est. 1824. (e) LUD-
WIGSBURG, Germany. Painted gold. 1816.

f   g   h   i   j

(f) CLIGNANCOURT, France. Hard paste. Est. 1771. (g) DERBY,
Great Britain. Hard paste. Painted red or violet. 1798. (h-i-j) SEV-
RES, France. Hard paste. 1700.

k   l   m   n   o

(k) POPPELSDORF, Germany. Fayence, porcelain. 1825. (l)
DERBY. Great Britain. Painted red, gold. 1811-1848. (m-n-o)
DERBY, Great Britain. 1784-1848.

a   b   c   d   e

(**a**) DERBY, Great Britain. William Duesbury. Porcelain. 1784-1810.
(**b-c**) DERBY, Great Britain. Duesbury and Kean. Porcelain. 1795.
(**d**) DERBY, Great Britain. Stevenson and Hancock. Hard paste.
Painted color. 1850-1870. (**e**) DERBY, Great Britain. Painted red,
gold. 1815-1830.

f   g   h   i   j

(**f**) DERBY, Great Britain. Circa 1800. (**g**) SEVRES, France. Hard
paste. 1814-1848. (**h**) VINCENNES, France. Hard paste. 1765.
(**i**) CLIGNANCOURT, France. Painted red. Est. 1771. (**j**) DERBY,
Great Britain. Royal Crown Derby, factory. Porcelain. 1876-1953.

k   l   m   n   o

(**k**) COPENHAGEN, Denmark. Royal Copenhagen, factory. Underglaze blue. 1905. (**l**) COPENHAGEN, Denmark. Royal Copenhagen. 1929. (**m**) COPENHAGEN, Denmark. Royal Copenhagen,
factory. Underglaze green, wavy lines blue. 1894. (**n**) COPEN-
HAGEN, Denmark. Royal Copenhagen, factory. Underglaze green,
wavy lines blue. 1923. (**o**) BELLEEK, Ireland. Est. 1863.

Powell & Bishop

a — b c d e

(a) FENTON, Great Britain. Crown Staffordshire Porcelain Company. 1870. (b) LONGTON, Great Britain. R. H. Plant and Company. Late 19th century. (c) HANLEY, Great Britain. Powell and Bishop. Impressed or printed. 1865-1878. (d-e) MARIEBERG, Sweden. Pottery and soft paste. Painted color. 1750.

f g h

(f) MARIEBERG, Sweden. Pottery and soft paste. 1766. (g) MARIEBERG, Sweden. Pottery and soft paste. November 24, 1764. (h) MARIEBERG, Sweden. Pottery and soft paste. October 14, 1768.

BELLEEK

i j k l m

(i) LONGTON, Great Britain. William Adderley and Company. After 1870. (j) BURSLEM, Great Britain. A. J. Wilkinson. Late 19th century. (k) LONGTON, Great Britain. Charles Allerton. After 1891. (l) TRENTON, New Jersey, U.S.A. Ott (Otter) and Brewer. 1876. (m) TRENTON, New Jersey, U.S.A. Burroughs and Mountford. 1879-1882.

a   **b**   **c**   **d**   **e**

(**a-b**) DERBY, Great Britain. Robert Bloor. 1811-1848. (**c**) SHEL-
TON, Great Britain. After 1891. (**d**) EVANSVILLE, Indiana, U.S.A.
Crown Pottery Company. Est. 1891. (**e**) FENTON, Great Britain.
Crown Staffordshire Porcelain Company. 1900.

f   **g**   **h**   **i**   **j**

(**f**) HANLEY, Great Britain. Robert Wilson, owner. 1786. (**g**)
LONGPORT, Great Britain. Davenport. Circa 1810. (**h**) DERBY,
Great Britain. Robert Bloor. Printed red. 1811-1848. (**i**) SWANSEA,
Great Britain. D. J. Evans and Company. 1859-1870. (**j**) DERBY,
Great Britain. 1760.

k   **l**   **m**   **n**   **o**

(**k-l-m**) DERBY, Great Britain. William Duesbury. 1760. (**n**) BAL-
TIMORE, Maryland, U.S.A. Edwin Bennett. 1856-1890. (**o**) COAL-
PORT, Great Britain. After 1891.

a b c d

(a) WORCESTER, Great Britain. Royal Service for the Duke of Clarence. Circa 1793. (b) WORCESTER, Great Britain. Hard paste. Painted color. 1793-1807. (c) GINORI, Italy. 18th century. (d) LIVERPOOL, Great Britain. Herculaneum. Impressed or printed. 1840.

e f g h

(e) GIESSHUBEL, Germany. Hamburger and Company. 19th century. (f) COBRIDGE, Great Britain. James Clews, potter. 1819-1829. (g) LIMOGES, France. Circa 1880. (h) GERMANY. Mid-19th century.

i j k l

(i) LUNEVILLE, France. Keller and Guerin, owner. Fayence. 1788. (j) FENTON, Great Britain. Ashworth. 1813-1851. (k) HANLEY, Great Britain. George Ashworth. After 1859. (l) STOKE-ON-TRENT, Great Britain. Minton, factory. Circa 1870.

a   b   c   d   e

(a) TRENTON, New Jersey, U.S.A. Ott (Otter) and Brewer. 1886. (b) SPAIN. 19th century. (c) EVANSVILLE, Indiana, U.S.A. Crown Pottery Company. Est. 1891. (d) TRENTON, New Jersey, U.S.A. Ott (Otter) and Brewer. 1886. (e) GREAT BRITAIN. After 1891.

f   g   h   i   j

(f) DERBY, Great Britain. Royal Crown Derby. Porcelain. 1890-1953. (g) STOKE-ON-TRENT, Great Britain. Cauldon Potteries Limited. 1891-1953. (h) DERBY, Great Britain. Royal Crown Derby. Porcelain. 1890. (i) BURSLEM, Great Britain. Wood, potter. After 1891. (j) TUNSTALL, Great Britain. T. G. and F. Booth. After 1891.

k   l   m   n   o

(k) EAST LIVERPOOL, Ohio, U.S.A. George Murphy Pottery Company. 19th century. (l) EAST LIVERPOOL, Ohio, U.S.A. Vodrey Brothers. Circa 1875. (m) SEBRING, Ohio, U.S.A. Sebring Pottery Company. Est. 1887. (n) FENTON, Great Britain. Crown Staffordshire Porcelain Company. Circa 1890. (o) TUNSTALL, Great Britain. Alfred Meakin. After 1891.

ROYAL SEMI-PORCELAIN
JOHN MADDOCK & SONS
ENGLAND.

TURNER.

W. DUESBURY.
1803.

WILSON

a   b   c   d

(a) BURSLEM, Great Britain. John Maddock and Sons. After 1891.
(b) LONGTON, Great Britain. John Turner. Est. 1872. (c) DERBY,
Great Britain. William Duesbury. Porcelain. 1803. (d) HANLEY,
Great Britain. Robert or David Wilson. 18th-19th century.

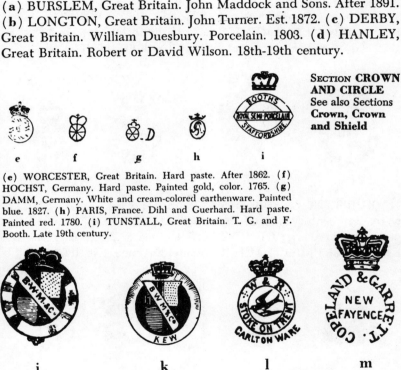

Section **CROWN
AND CIRCLE**
See also Sections
**Crown, Crown
and Shield**

e   f   g   h   i

(e) WORCESTER, Great Britain. Hard paste. After 1862. (f)
HOCHST, Germany. Hard paste. Painted gold, color. 1765. (g)
DAMM, Germany. White and cream-colored earthenware. Painted
blue. 1827. (h) PARIS, France. Dihl and Guerhard. Hard paste.
Painted red. 1780. (i) TUNSTALL, Great Britain. T. G. and F.
Booth. Late 19th century.

j   k   l   m

(j) SHELTON, Great Britain. T. C. Brown, Westhead, Moore, and
Company. 1858. (k) SHELTON, Great Britain. T. C. Brown, West-
head, Moore, and Company. After 1859. (l) STOKE-ON-TRENT,
Great Britain. Wiltshaw and Robinson. Late 19th century. (m)
STOKE-ON-TRENT, Great Britain. Spode, factory. Bone porcelain.
1833-1847.

a   b   c   d

(a) STOKE-ON-TRENT, Great Britain. W. T. Copeland and Sons. Spode factory. Bone porcelain. 1833-1847. (b) COBRIDGE, Great Britain. 1814. (c) LAMBETH, Great Britain. Doulton, factory. Est. 1872. (d) LAMBETH, Great Britain. Doulton, factory. 1891.

e   f   g   h

(e) BURSLEM, Great Britain. E. Bourne and J. E. Leigh. Earthenware. 19th century. (f) GREAT BRITAIN. Bates, Elliot, and Company. Est. 1790. (g) GRUNSTADT. Germany. White earthenware. Est. 1801. (h) METTLACH, Germany. Fayence. Est. 1809.

i   j   k   l   m

(i) METTLACH, Germany. Fayence. Est. 1809. (j) HANLEY, Great Britain. J. G. Meakin. After 1891. (k) BURSLEM, Great Britain. John Maddock and Sons. Earthenware. After 1891. (l) SHELTON, Great Britain. Job Ridgways, potter. Stone china, porcelain. Est. 1802. (m) EAST LIVERPOOL, Ohio, U.S.A. Knowles, Taylor, and Knowles. Est. 1854.

a   b   c   d   e

(**a**) BOHEMIA. Fischern. 1848. (**b**) GREENPOINT, New York, U.S.A. Faience Manufacturing Company. Printed. 1880-1892. (**c**) EAST LIVERPOOL, Ohio, U.S.A. Globe Pottery Company. Est. 1888. (**d**) SHELTON, Great Britain. Job Ridgways. After 1891. (**e**) TRENTON, New Jersey, U.S.A. Glasgow Pottery Company. Circa 1875.

f   g   h   i

(**f**) DERBY, Great Britain. Stevenson, Sharp and Company. After 1860. (**g**) TRENTON, New Jersey, U.S.A. Thomas Maddock and Sons. Est. 1882. (**h-i**) SHELTON, Great Britain. Job Ridgways, potter. After 1802.

j   k   l   m   n

(**j**) TUNSTALL, Great Britain. Printed. After 1891. (**k**) TEINITZ, Bohemia. Lead glazed earthenware. Est. 1801. (**l**) COPENHAGEN, Denmark. Royal Copenhagen, factory. Porcelain. Underglaze green, wavy lines blue. 1923. (**m**) COPENHAGEN, Denmark. Royal Copenhagen, factory. Porcelain. Underglaze green, wavy lines blue. 1897. (**n**) COPENHAGEN, Denmark. Royal Copenhagen, factory. Porcelain. Overglaze green or red. 1890.

a   b   c   d

(**a**) COPENHAGEN, Denmark. Royal Copenhagen, factory.Printed blue. 1889. (**b**) LONGTON, Great Britain. James Kent. 20th century. (**c**) STOKE-ON-TRENT, Great Britain. Minton, factory. 1888-1911. (**d**) STOKE-ON-TRENT, Great Britain. Minton, factory. 1911-1953.

e   f   g   h

(**e**) GREAT BRITAIN. Johnson Brothers. Est. 1883. (**f**) PARIS, France. Rue de Bondy, factory. Hard paste. Est. 1780. (**g**) GIESS-HUBEL, Bohemia. Porcelain. After 1891. (**h**) STOKE-ON-TRENT, Great Britain. W. T. Copeland and Sons. Spode, factory. 1833-1847.

i   j   k   l   m

(**i**) SEVRES, France. Hard paste. Painted blue. 1829. (**j**) DERBY, Great Britain. William Duesbury. Circa 1760. (**k**) COBRIDGE, Great Britain. Andrew Stevenson, potter. 1810-1818. (**l**) DERBY, Great Britain. Hard paste. Printed color. 1811-1848. (**m**) WORCES-TER, Great Britain. Robert Chamberlain and Son. Porcelain. 1850.

a b c d e

(**a**) EAST LIVERPOOL, Ohio, U.S.A. East End Pottery Company.
19th century. (**b**) BALTIMORE, Maryland, U.S.A. D. F. Haynes
and Company. Est. 1879. (**c**) LIVERPOOL, Great Britain. Herculaneum. Impressed or printed. 1800-1841. (**d**) STOKE-ON-TRENT,
Great Britain. Minton, factory. After 1868. (**e**) TRENTON, New
Jersey, U.S.A. Burgess and Campbell. Est. 1879.

f g h i j

(**f**) COBRIDGE, Great Britain. James Clews, potter. Blue printed
earthenware. 1819-1829. (**g**) SEVRES, France. Hard paste, soft
paste. 1845. (**h**) SEVRES, France. Hard paste, soft paste. 1848.
(**i**) SEVRES, France. Hard paste. Printed blue. 1848. (**j**) BALTI-
MORE, Maryland, U.S.A. D. F. Haynes and Company. Est. 1879.

k l m n

(**k**) BALTIMORE, Maryland, U.S.A. Bennett Pottery Company.
Est. 1840. (**l**) SAINT PETERSBURG, Russia. 1855-1881. (**m**) SEV-
RES, France. Hard paste for Catherine II of Russia. 1778. (**n**)
WORCESTER, Great Britain. Hard paste. Printed. 1800.

a   b   c   d

(a) STOKE-ON-TRENT, Great Britain. W. T. Copeland and Sons.
Spode, factory. After 1847. (b) FENTON, Great Britain. Crown
Staffordshire Porcelain Company. 1890. (c) MINTON, Great Brit-
ain. 20th century. (d) BALTIMORE, Maryland, U.S.A. Edwin
Bennett. 1856-1890.

Section **CROWN
AND SHIELD**
See also Sections
**Crown, Crown
and Circle**

e   f   g   h   i

(e) GERMANY. Painted blue. 19th century. (f) EISENBERG,
Germany. Earthenware. 19th century. (g) HEREND, Hungary.
Moritz Fischer, founder. Blue overglaze. 19th-20th century. (h-i)
SARREGUEMINES, France. Fayence, porcelain. 19th century.

 AL

j   k   l   m   n

(j) BOHEMIA. Porcelain. 1880. (k) GERMANY. Impressed. 1880.
(l) LUXEMBOURG, Belgium. 18th century. (m) THURINGIA,
Germany. Rudolstadt, factory. Impressed or stamped. 19th century.
(n) SARREGUEMINES, France. Fayence, porcelain. 19th century.

a   b   c   d   e

(a) MORAVIA, Germany. Frain, factory. Earthenware. 1799-1882.
(b) RUDOLSTADT, Germany. Impressed or stamped. 19th century. (c) VALOGNES, France. Hard paste. Est. 1793. (d) LONGTON, Great Britain. Hilditch and Son. 1795-1830. (e) GERMANY. Est. 1840.

f   g   h   i   j

(f) LUNEVILLE, France. Keller and Guerin. Fayence. After 1891.
(g) TRENTON, New Jersey, U.S.A. Mercer Pottery Company. Est.
1868. (h) GERMANY. Fayence. Est. 1882. (i) NIDERVILLER,
France. Fayence, porcelain. Circa 1830. (j) SARREGUEMINES,
France. Fayence, porcelain. 19th century.

k   l   m   n   o

(k) GERMANY. Est. 1835. (l) BAYERN, Germany. Paul Muller.
Hard paste. 1890-1917. (m) TIRSCHENREUTH, Germany. 1838-
1927. (n) STOKE-ON-TRENT, Great Britain. Pointons. 19th century. (o) BONN, Germany. F. A. Mehlem, factory. Est. 1836.

a   b   c   d

(a) BURSLEM, Great Britain. T. and R. Boote. Earthenware. After
1891. (b) STOKE-ON-TRENT, Great Britain. S. Fielding and Company. After 1891. (c) ELBOGEN, Germany. Springer and Company. Earthenware, porcelain. Est. 1815. (d) LONGTON, Great
Britain. Foley China Factory. After 1891.

e   f   g   h

(e) KLOSTERLE, Germany. Porcelain, lead-glazed earthenware.
Est. 1793. (f) HANLEY, Great Britain. After 1891. (g) BURSLEM,
Great Britain. Wilkinson. After 1891. (h) ZELL, Germany. Fayence.
Circa 1850.

SECTION **FLEUR
DE LIS**
See also Section
Lines

i   j   k   l   m   n

(i-j) BUEN RETIRO, Spain. Soft paste. 1759-1808. (k-l) NAPLES,
Italy. Capo-di-Monte, factory. Soft paste. Painted blue. 1736 (moved
to Buen Retiro, Spain, 1759). (m-n) MARSEILLES, France. Fayence. Printed color. 1777.

a   b   c   d   e   f

(a) MARSEILLES, France. Fayence. Printed color. 1777. (b-c) STOKE-ON-TRENT, Great Britain. Minton, factory. Painted green. After 1850. (d) ROUEN, France. Fayence. Painted color. 16th century. (e-f) MARSEILLES, France. Fayence. Printed color. 1777.

g   h   i   j   k   l

(g) BOW, Great Britain. Soft paste. Painted blue. 1730. (h) ROUEN, France. Fayence. 17th century. (i) SAINT CLOUD, France. Soft paste. Impressed. 1680-1766. (j) GINORI, Italy. Painted blue. After 1820. (k-l) BUEN RETIRO, Spain. Soft paste. 1759-1808.

m   n   o   p   q   r

(m) BUEN RETIRO, Spain. Soft paste. 1759-1808. (n) GINORI, Italy. Painted blue. After 1820. (o) BUEN RETIRO, Spain. Soft paste. 1759-1808. (p) ORLEANS, France. 1753-1812. (q) EAST LIVERPOOL, Ohio. U.S.A. Sevres China Company. Est. 1900. (r) BUEN RETIRO, Spain. Soft paste. 1759-1808.

a   b   c   d

(a) EAST LIVERPOOL, Ohio, U.S.A. Sevres China Company. Est.
1900. (b) LOWESBY, Great Britain. Earthenware. Impressed. Est.
1835. (c) LOWESBY, Great Britain. 1835. (d) EAST LIVERPOOL,
Ohio, U.S.A. Sevres China Company. Est. 1900.

e   f   g   h

(e) BUEN RETIRO, Spain. Soft paste. 1759-1808. (f) SEVRES,
France. Hard paste. Painted blue. 1830. (g) EAST LIVERPOOL,
Ohio, U.S.A. Sevres China Company. Est. 1900. (h) DETROIT,
Michigan, U.S.A. 19th century.

Section **FLOWER
AND TREE**
See also Sections
**Circle and Sign,
Shield, Square**

i.   j   k   l   m

(i) LONGPORT, Great Britain. Circa 1825. (j) HOLLAND. De
Roos (The Rose). Fayence. Delft. 1764. (k) TYLERSPORT, Penn-
sylvania, U.S.A. Circa 1830. (l) EAST LIVERPOOL, Ohio, U.S.A.
Circa 1840. (m) TYLERSPORT, Pennsylvania, U.S.A. Michael
School (Scholl). Impressed. Circa 1830.

a b c d e

(a) BOSTON, Massachusetts, U.S.A. New England Pottery Company. Est. 1875. (b-c) HOLLAND. De Roos (The Rose). Fayence. Delft. Painted blue. 1764. (d) CAUGHLEY, Great Britain. Rose and Company. Hard paste. Painted color. 1799. (e) COALPORT, Great Britain. 19th century.

f g h i

(f-g-h-i) HOLLAND. De Roos (The Rose). Fayence. Delft. 1675.

j k l m n

(j) HOHENSTEIN, Germany. After 1822. (k) FULHAM, Great Britain. 1888. (l) BOSTON, Massachusetts, U.S.A. Grueby Faience Company. Est. 1897. (m) IMENAU, Germany. Fayence, porcelain. Est. 1777. (n) THURINGIA, Germany. Limbach, factory. Porcelain. Est. 1772.

a	**b**	**c**	**d**	**e**

(**a**) THURINGIA, Germany. Volkstedt, factory. Porcelain. Est. 1760. (**b-c**) GROSBREITENBACH, Germany. Hard paste. Painted color. 1770. (**d**) CHELSEA, Massachusetts, U.S.A. Chelsea Keramic Art Works. Circa 1890. (**e**) TRENTON, New Jersey, U.S.A. Cook Pottery Company. Circa 1900.

f	**g**	**h**	**i**	**j**

(**f**) BEAVER FALLS, Pennsylvania, U.S.A. Mayer Pottery Company. Est. 1881. (**g-h**) TRENTON, New Jersey, U.S.A. John Maddock and Sons. After 1894. (**i**) BERLIN, Germany. Hard paste. Painted blue, green, gold. Often on damaged pieces. 1800. (**j**) HOLLAND. Fayence. Delft. 18th century.

k	**l**	**m**	**n**

(**k**) HOLLAND. De Ster (The Star). Fayence. Delft. 1720. (**l-m-n**) CAMBRIDGE, Ohio, U.S.A. Cambridge Art Pottery Company. 19th century.

a   b   c   d   e

SECTION **LINES**
See also Sections
**E, F, H, I, K, L,
M, N, S, T, V, W,
X-Y, Anchor,
Arrow, Copies of
Oriental Marks**

(a) ALTHALDENSLEBEN, Germany. Hard Paste. Impressed. Blue. Circa 1800. (b) SAINT PETERSBURG, Russia. Hard paste. Painted blue. Est. 1744. (c) COPENHAGEN, Denmark. Royal Copenhagen, factory. 1830-1845. (d) LUDWIGSBURG, Germany. Hard paste. Painted red or blue. 1758. (e) COPENHAGEN, Denmark. Royal Copenhagen, factory. 1775.

f   g   h   i   j

(f) VARAGES, France. Fayence. 1770. (g) GINORI, Italy. Capo-di-monte, factory. Blue. 1743-1821. (h) LEEDS, Great Britain. Painted color. 1770. (i-j) BRISTOL, Great Britain. Porcelain. Painted color. Circa 1770.

k   l   m   n   o

(k-l) VARAGES, France. Fayence. Painted black or red. 1730. (m) FULDA, Germany. Fayence. Underglaze blue. 1765-1780. (n) GOULT, France. Fayence. 1740. (o) VINOVO, Italy. Porcelain. Painted black. 1776-1820.

a   b   c   d   e

(**a**) FULDA, Germany. Fayence, hard paste. Painted blue. 1765.
(**b**) BRISTOL, Great Britain. Porcelain. 1750. (**c**) CHELSEA,
Great Britain. Porcelain. 1745-1784. (**d**) VARAGES. France. Fayence. Painted black, blue, red. 1730. (**e**) TURIN, Italy. Porcelain.
Est. 1737.

f   g   h   i   j

(**f**) NYMPHENBURG, Germany. Porcelain. Impressed, incised.
Est. 1755. (**g**) FAENZA, Italy. Fayence. 16th century. (**h**) BUEN
RETIRO, Spain. Soft paste. 1759-1808. (**i-j**) BOW, Great Britain.
Porcelain. 1750.

k   l   m   n   o

(**k-l**) LONGTON, Great Britain. William Littler, potter. Porcelain,
stoneware. 1750-1760. (**m**) URBINO, Italy. Fayence. 16th century.
(**n**) BOW, Great Britain. Porcelain. 1750. (**o**) WEESP, Holland.
Porcelain. Est. 1759.

a b c d e

(a) WEESP, Holland. Porcelain. Est. 1759. (b) LIMBACH, Germany. Porcelain. Painted red, black, purple. 1772-1778. (c) PLYMOUTH, Great Britain. Hard paste. Painted blue, red, gold. 1768. (d) BORDEAUX, France. Fayence, porcelain. Painted gold, blue. Est. 1781. (e) LIMBACH, Germany. Porcelain. Painted red, black, purple. 1772-1788.

f g h i j

(f) BOW, Great Britain. Porcelain. 1750. (g) PARIS, France. De La Courtille, factory. Hard paste. 1773. (h) BRISTOL, Great Britain. Porcelain. Est. 1750. (i) GERMANY. 1863. (j) MEISSEN, Germany. Circa 1724.

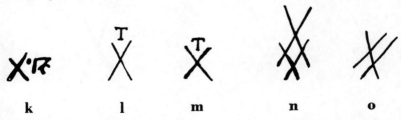

k l m n o

(k) BRISTOL, Great Britain. Porcelain. Est. 1750. (l-m) MEISSEN, Germany. Carl Thieme. 19th century. (n) MEISSEN, Germany. Herold, manager. Hard paste. Painted blue. 1720. (o) SITZENDORF, Germany. Imitation Meissen porcelain. Est. 1850.

a   b   c   d   e

(a) BOURG-LA-REINE, France. Hard paste. 1773. (b) MOUS-
TIERS, France. Fayence. 1721. (c) NYMPHENBURG, Germany.
Porcelain. Impressed or incised. Est. 1755. (d) CASEMENÉ,
France. Fayence. Impressed. 1800. (e) COPENHAGEN, Denmark.
Est. 1772.

f   g   h   i   j

(f) COPENHAGEN, Denmark. Hard paste. Painted color. 1772
(mark uncertain). (g-h) ROUEN, France. Fayence. Circa 1740.
(i-j) TRENTON, New Jersey, U.S.A. Burgess and Campbell. Est.
1879.

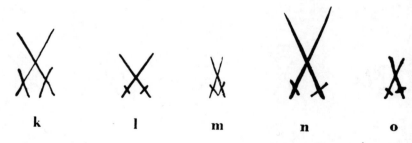

k   l   m   n   o

(k) MEISSEN, Germany. Hard paste. 1818-1924. (l) WORCES-
TER, Great Britain. Hard paste. Circa 1780. (m-n) MEISSEN, Ger-
many. Hard paste. Painted blue. 1726. (o) BRISTOL, Great Britain.
Porcelain. 1816-1835.

(a) DERBY, Great Britain. Porcelain. 1745-1848. (b) WORCES-
TER, Great Britain. Dr. Wall. Porcelain. 1751-1783. (c) MEISSEN,
Germany. Hard paste. Painted blue. 1725-1763. (d) MEISSEN, Ger-
many. Hard paste. Painted blue. After 1924. (e) BRISTOL, Great
Britain. Pottery, porcelain. 1750.

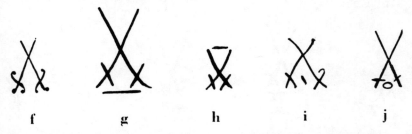

(f) MEISSEN, Germany. Hard paste. 1724. (g-h) MEISSEN, Germany. Hard paste. Defective porcelain. Painted blue and scratched.
1760. (i-j) MEISSEN, Germany. Hard paste. 1763-1774.

(k) MEISSEN, Germany. Marcolini period. Hard paste. 1774-1814.
(l-m-n-o) BRISTOL, Great Britain. Porcelain. Painted blue, gold.
1770-1781.

a   **b**   **c**   **d**   **e**

(a) WORCESTER. Great Britain. Dr. Wall. Porcelain. 1751-1783.
(b-c-d) BRISTOL, Great Britain. Porcelain. Painted blue, gold.
1770-1781. (e) WORCESTER, Great Britain. Dr. Wall. Porcelain.
1751-1783.

f   **g**   **h**   **i**   **j**

(f-g). MEISSEN, Germany. Hard paste. 1818. (h-i) BRISTOL,
Great Britain. Pottery, porcelain. Painted blue, gold. 1770-1781.
(j) WALLENDORF, Germany. Porcelain. 1776.

k   **l**   **m**   **n**   **o**

(k-l) MEISSEN, Germany. Bruhl, manager. Hard paste. Painted
blue. 1750. (m) MEISSEN, Germany. Herold, manager. Hard paste.
Painted blue. 1739. (n) DORNHEIM. Germany. 19th century.
(o) MEISSEN, Germany. Hard paste. Painted blue. 1814-1818.

a   b   c   d   e

(a) MEISSEN, Germany. Konigliche Porzellen Manufactur. Hard paste. Painted blue. 1723. (b) MEISSEN, Germany. Meissen Porzellen Manufactur. Hard paste. Painted blue. 1723. (c) BRISTOL, Great Britain. Pottery, porcelain. Painted blue, gold. 1770-1781. (d) RAUENSTEIN, Germany. Porcelain. Painted blue, red, black, purple. Est. 1783. (e) MEISSEN, Germany. Hard paste. Painted blue. 1745-1763.

f   g   h   i   j

(f-g) PARIS, France. Samson the imitator. 1875. (h-i) CAUGHLEY, Great Britain. Hard paste. Painted blue. 1750. (j) COALPORT, Great Britain. Porcelain. 1796.

k   l   m   n   o

(k-l) TOURNAY, Belgium. Porcelain, fayence. Est. 1751. (m) WEESP, Holland. Porcelain. Painted blue. Est. 1764. (n) MEISSEN, Germany. Hard paste. Circa 1725. (o) WORCESTER, Great Britain. Soft paste, hard paste. Painted blue, red. 1750.

(**a-b-c-d-e**) MEISSEN, Germany. Hard paste, imperfect pieces. Painted blue, scratched. 1760.

(**f-g-h-i-j**) MEISSEN, Germany. Hard paste, imperfect pieces. Painted blue, scratched. 1760.

(**k-l-m**) BRISTOL, Great Britain. Porcelain. 1750. (**n**) WEST SMETHWICK, Great Britain. Ruskin pottery. 20th century. (**o**) DOROTHEENTHAL, Germany. Fayence. Est. 1707.

a   b   c   d   e

(a) DOROTHEENTHAL, Germany. Fayence. Painted color. Est. 1707. (**b-c-d-e**) VINCENNES, France. Pierre Antoine Hannong, founder. Hard paste. 1765.

f   g   h   i   j

(f) MONTREUIL, France. Tinet, potter. 1815-1873. (g) PARIS, France. Jacob Petit. Hard paste. 1820. (**h-i**) MEISSEN, Germany. Hard paste. Painted blue. 1725-1730. (j) ANSBACH, Bavaria. Hard paste. Est. 1708.

k   l   m   n   o

(k) WEESP, Holland. Hard paste. Est. 1759. (l) ANSBACH, Bavaria. Hard paste. Est. 1708. (m) SAVONA, Italy. 18th century. (n) BRISTOL, Great Britain. Porcelain. Est. 1770. (o) RUDOLSTADT, Germany. Hard paste. Painted blue. 1720.

a　　　　　b　　　　　c　　　　　d　　　　　e

(a) MEISSEN, Germany. Herold, manager. Hard paste. Painted blue. 1730. (b) WEESP, Holland. Hard paste. Est. 1759. (c) MEISSEN, Germany. Herold, manager. Hard paste. Painted blue. 1730. (d-e) RUDOLSTADT, Germany. Hard paste. Painted blue. 1720.

f　　　　　g　　　　　h　　　　　i　　　　　j

(f-g-h) VOLKSTEDT, Germany. Porcelain. 1760. (i) BOW, Great Britain. Porcelain. 1750. (j) CHELSEA, Great Britain. Porcelain. 1745-1784.

k　　　　　l　　　　　m　　　　　n　　　　　o

(k-l-m) SWANSEA, Great Britain. Hard paste. Impressed. 1814. (n-o) THURINGIA, Germany. Limbach, factory. Porcelain. Est. 1772.

a   b   c   d   e

(a) MEISSEN, Germany. Hard paste. 19th century. (b) WALLEN-
DORF, Germany. Porcelain. Painted blue. Est. 1764. (c) LONG-
TON, Great Britain. William Littler, potter. Porcelain, stoneware.
1750-1760. (d) THURINGIA, Germany. Limbach, factory. Porcelain. Est. 1772. (e) WORCESTER, Great Britain. Porcelain. Painted
blue. Est. 1751.

f   g   h   i   j

(f) CAUGHLEY, Great Britain. Thomas Turner, potter. Hard paste.
Painted blue. 1772. (g-h) RAUENSTEIN, Germany. Porcelain.
Painted blue, purple, red. Est. 1783. (i) SAINT PETERSBURG,
Russia. Hard paste. Painted blue. 1762. (j) SAINT PETERSBURG,
Russia. Paul Korniloffe. Hard paste. Painted. 1762.

k   l   m   n   o

(k) THURINGIA, Germany. Ilmenau, factory. Fayence, porcelain.
Est. 1777. (l-m-n) TOURS, France. Fayence, hard paste. Painted
blue. 1840. (o) BUEN RETIRO, Spain. Soft paste. 1759-1808.

a   b   c   d   e

(**a**) NIDERVILLER, France. Hard paste. 1770-1793. (**b**) LUD-WIGSBURG, Germany. Hard paste. 1758-1793. (**c-d**) NIDERVIL-LER, France. Hard paste. 1770-1793. (**e**) NUREMBURG. Germany. Fayence. Est. 1712.

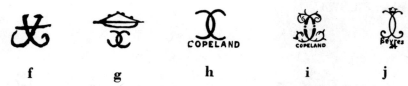

f   g   h   i   j

(**f**) ILMENAU, Germany. Porcelain. Est. 1777. (**g**) NIDERVIL-LER, France. Hard paste. 1770-1793. (**h-i**) STOKE-ON-TRENT, Great Britain. W. T. Copeland. Porcelain. 1833. (**j**) SEVRES, France. Porcelain. 1824-1828.

k   l   m   n   o

(**k-l-m-n**) SEVRES, France. Porcelain. 1824-1828. (**o**) LUDWIGS-BURG, Germany. Hard paste. Painted blue, red. 1758-1793.

a　　　　b　　　　c　　　　d　　　　e

(**a**) BUEN RETIRO, Spain. Soft paste. 1759-1808. (**b**) FON-
TAINEBLEAU, France. Hard paste. After 1875. (**c**) STOKE-ON-
TRENT, Great Britain. Minton, factory. Hard paste. Painted blue,
red. 1790. (**d**) PARIS, France. Gros Caillou, factory. Hard paste.
Painted color. 1773. (**e**) SEVRES, France. Soft paste. 1745-1753.

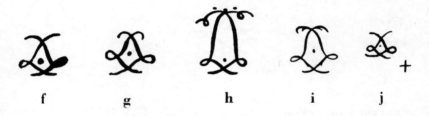

f　　　　g　　　　h　　　　i　　　　j

(**f-g-h-i**) SEVRES, France. Soft paste. 1745-1753. (**j**) COALPORT,
Great Britain. Porcelain. Est. 1796.

k　　　　l　　　　m　　　　n　　　　o

(**k**) SEVRES, France. Soft paste. 1745-1753. (**l**) WORCESTER,
Great Britain. Hard paste. 1751-1783. (**m**) SEVRES, France. Soft
paste. 1745-1753. (**n-o**) SAINT AMAND, France. Fayence, soft
paste. 1711-1778.

a   b   c   d   e

(a) STOKE-ON-TRENT, Great Britain. Minton, factory. Bone
china. 18th century to 1831. (b) SEVRES, France. Soft paste. 1745-
1753. (c) SEVRES, France. Soft paste. 1753. (d) SEVRES, France.
Soft paste. 1778. (e) SEVRES, France. Soft paste. Circa 1753.

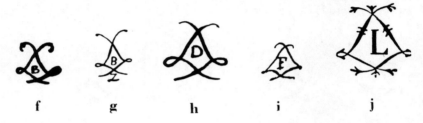

f   g   h   i   j

(f-g) SEVRES, France. Soft paste. 1754. (h) SEVRES, France.
Soft paste. 1756. (i) FRANCE. Feuillet, decorator. Painted gold,
black. 1820-1850. (j) SEVRES, France. Soft paste, hard paste. 1764.

k   l   m   n

(k) SEVRES, France. Soft paste, hard paste. 1790. (l) SEVRES,
France. Hard paste, soft paste. 1771. (m) SEVRES, France. Hard
paste, soft paste. 1821. (n) SEVRES, France. Hard paste, soft paste.
1770.

a   b   c   d

(**a**) SEVRES, France. Soft paste. 1745-1753. (**b**) SEVRES, France. Soft paste. 1745-1753. (**c**) SEVRES, France. Soft paste, hard paste. 1745-1753. (**d**) STOKE-ON-TRENT, Great Britain. E. Brain and Company Limited. Foley China Company. 19th century.

e   f   g   h   i   j

(**e**) COBRIDGE, Great Britain. William Brownfield. Circa 1850. (**f-g**) TRENTON, New Jersey, U.S.A. Willetts Manufacturing Company. Est. 1879. (**h-i-j**) BOW, Great Britain. Porcelain. Painted red, blue. 1750.

k   l   m   n   o   p

(**k**) BOW, Great Britain. Porcelain. 1750. (**l**) BUEN RETIRO, Spain. Soft paste. 1759-1808. (**m-n-o-p**) MEISSEN, Germany. Hard paste. Painted blue. 1710; or WORCESTER, Great Britain. Soft paste. Painted blue. 1753.

(**a-b-c-d-e**) BERLIN, Germany. Royal factory. Hard paste. Painted blue. 1760. (**f**) RUSSIA. Fayence. 1845.

(**g**) BERLIN, Germany. Royal factory. Hard paste. Painted blue. 1760. (**h**) HANLEY, Great Britain. 19th century. (**i**) NYMPHEN-BURG, Germany. Porcelain. Impressed or incised. Est. 1747. (**j**) PREMIERES, France. Fayence. 19th century. (**k**) HOLLAND. Red earthenware. 1678.

(**l**) CAUGHLEY, Great Britain. Hard paste. Painted blue. 1750. (**m**) BOW, Great Britain. Porcelain. 1750. (**n**) BOURG-LA-REINE, France. Porcelain. 1773. (**o**) BRISTOL, Great Britain. Hard paste. Painted color. 1770. (**p**) NIDERVILLER, France. Fayence, porcelain. 1754.

a   b   c   d   e   f   g

(**a-b**) BADEN BADEN, Germany. Hard paste. Painted gold, color. 1753. (**c-d-e-f**) HOLLAND. De Porceleyne Byl (The Porcelain Hatchet). Fayence. Delft. 1759. (**g**) PIRKENHAMMER, Germany. Hard paste. 1850.

SECTION **MIS-CELLANEOUS**

h   i   j

(**h-i**) BURSLEM, Great Britain. T. and R. Boote. Late 18th century. (**j**) COBRIDGE, Great Britain. Staffordshire. Painted blue. 1800.

k   l   m   n   o

(**k-l**) HOLLAND. De Klauw (The Claw). Fayence. Delft. 1764. (**m**) LUDWIGSBURG, Germany. Porcelain. 1756-1824. (**n-o**) HOLLAND. De Klauw (The Claw). Fayence. Delft. 1764.

a   b   c   d   e

(**a-b-c-d-e**) HOLLAND. De Klauw (The Claw). Fayence. Delft. 1764.

f   g   h   i   j

(**f**) JERSEY CITY. New Jersey, U.S.A. American Pottery Manufacturing Company. Printed. Circa 1835. (**g-h**) EAST LIVERPOOL, Ohio, U.S.A. Burford Brothers Pottery Company. 1879-1900. (**i**) HANLEY, Great Britain. J. H. Weatherby and Son. After 1891. (**j**) STEUBENVILLE, Ohio, U.S.A. Steubenville Pottery Company. Est. 1887.

k   l   m   n

(**k**) WHEELING, West Virginia, U.S.A. Wheeling Pottery Company. Est. 1879. (**l**) KLOSTERLE, Bohemia. Porcelain, lead-glazed earthenware. 1793. (**m**) LIMOGES, France. Fayence, porcelain. 19th century. (**n**) STOKE-ON-TRENT, Great Britain. Spode, factory. W. T. Copeland and Sons. 1847-1891.

a   b   c   d   e

(a) WORCESTER, Great Britain. Blueware. 1751-1800. (b) STEU-BENVILLE. Ohio, U.S.A. Lonhuda Pottery. Est. 1892. (c) MON-MOUTH, Illinois, U.S.A. Monmouth Pottery Company. Circa 1890. (d) HOLLAND. Fayence. Delft. 18th century. (e) HOLLAND. De Oude Moriaan's Hooft (The Old Moor's Head). Fayence. Delft. 1680.

f   g   h   i   j

(f) GERMANY. 1842. (g) ELBOGEN, Germany. Earthenware, porcelain. Est. 1815. (h) VIENNA, Austria. Royal Vienna, factory. Circa 1850. (i) BOSTON, Massachusetts, U.S.A. New England Pottery Company. Circa 1887. (j) NEW YORK, New York, U.S.A. Carr and Morrison. Circa 1860.

k   l   m   n

(k-l-m-n) DERBY, Great Britain. Hard paste. Painted blue. 1745-1848.

a   b   c

(**a**) STEUBENVILLE, Ohio, U.S.A. Steubenville Pottery Company.
Est. 1879. (**b**) PARIS, France. Hard paste. Painted gold. 1870.
(**c**) WELLSVILLE, Ohio, U.S.A. J.H. Baum. Printed. 1880.

d   e   f   g   h

(**d**) MONTE LUPO, Italy. Pottery. 17th century. (**e-f**) TRENTON,
New Jersey, U.S.A. Cook Pottery Company. Circa 1900. (**g**) EAST
LIVERPOOL, Ohio, U.S.A. Globe Pottery Company. Est. 1888.
(**h**) BOSTON, Massachusetts, U.S.A. New England Pottery Company. 1886.

i   j   k   l   m

(**i**) EAST LIVERPOOL, Ohio, U.S.A. West End Pottery Company.
Est. 1893. (**j**) DIRMSTEIN, Germany. Fayence, earthenware. Est.
1778-1788. (**k**) CAUGHLEY, Great Britain. Porcelain. 1750-1814.
(**l**) HOLLAND. Fayence. Delft. Painted red. 1700. (**m**) CLIG-
NANCOURT, France. Hard paste. 1771-1775.

a   b   c   d   e

(a) WORCESTER, Great Britain. 1751-1783. (b-c-d-e) CHAN-
TILLY, France. Soft paste. Painted blue, red. 1725-1800.

f   g   h   i   j

(f) SCOTLAND. J. and M. P. Bell and Company. After 1842.
(g) LIMOGES, France. Fayence, hard paste. 1736-1796. (h)
TRENTON, New Jersey, U.S.A. Bellmark Pottery Company. Est.
1893. (i-j) HULL, Great Britain. Bellevue Pottery Company. Earthenware. 1825.

k   l   m   n

(k) HULL, Great Britain. Bellevue Pottery Company. Earthenware.
1825. (l) SAVONO, Italy. 17th century. (m) SWANSEA. Great
Britain. Cambrian, factory. Soft paste. 1765. (n) STOKE-ON-
TRENT, Great Britain. Spode, factory. W. T. Copeland and Sons.
Porcelain. 1847.

SECTION
NUMBERS
See also Section
Lines

a   b   c   d   e   f

(**a**) BRISTOL, Great Britain. Pottery, porcelain. Painted blue, gold. 18th century. (**b**) PLYMOUTH, Great Britain. Hard paste. Painted red, blue, gold. 1768. (**c**) BRISTOL, Great Britain. Pottery, porcelain. Painted blue, gold. 18th century. (**d**) TRENTON, New Jersey, U.S.A. Isaac Broome. Est. 1880. (**e**) BRISTOL, Great Britain. Pottery, porcelain. Painted blue, gold. 18th century. (**f**) NEVERS, France. Pottery. Painted color. 16th century.

g   h   i   j   k

(**g-h**) PLYMOUTH, Great Britain. Hard paste. Painted red, gold, blue. 1768. (**i**) BRISTOL, Great Britain. Porcelain. 1770-1781. (**j-k**) PLYMOUTH, Great Britain. Painted red, gold, blue. 1768.

l   m   n   o   p

(**l**) BRISTOL, Great Britain. Porcelain. Painted blue, gold. 1770-1781. (**m**) TOURNAY, Belgium. Fayence. 1850. (**n**) BRISTOL, Great Britain. Porcelain, pottery. Painted blue, gold. 1770-1781. (**o**) BUEN RETIRO, Spain. Hard paste. 1804-1808. (**p**) BRISTOL, Great Britain. Pottery, porcelain. Painted blue, gold. 1770-1781.

a
b
c

(a) YEARSLEY, Great Britain. Green-glazed earthenware. 18th century. (b) HOLLAND. De Ster (The Star). Fayence. Delft. 1720. (c) HOLLAND. De Porceleyne Schootel (The Porcelain Dish). Fayence. Delft. 1759.

d
e
f
g

(d) LESUM, Germany. Fayence. 1755-1800. (e) BUEN RETIRO, Spain. Soft paste. 1759-1808. (f) BRISTOL, Great Britain. Porcelain. 1770-1781. (g) VINOVO, Italy. Porcelain. Painted. 1776-1820.

Section RUSSIAN LETTERS

$\overset{\displaystyle\mathcal{E}}{*}$

А| Ā   П:К.   ВРАТЬЕВЪ
Корниловыхъ   ГАРДНЕРЪ

h   i   j   k   l

(h) MOSCOW, Russia. A. Popoff, owner. 1800-1872. (i) MOSCOW, Russia. A. Gardner. Hard paste. Painted color. 1750. (j) SAINT PETERSBURG, Russia. 1762-1796. (k) SAINT PETERSBURG, Russia. Hard paste. Printed. 1825. (l) MOSCOW, Russia. A. Gardner. Hard-paste. Painted color. 1750.

ΦΓ
ГУЛИНА   ПОПОВЫ   *Baranǿwka*

·a   b   c

(a) MOSCOW, Russia. Hard paste, fayence. Impressed. Circa 1800.
(b) MOSCOW, Russia. A. Popoff. Hard paste. Painted color. 1830.
(c) BARANOVKA, Poland. Porcelain. Painted black, brown. 1801-1895.

SECTION **SHIELD**
See also Sections
Circle and Sign,
Crown and Circle,
Crown and Shield,
Square

d   e   f   g.   h   i

(d-e-f-g) VIENNA, Austria. Royal Vienna, factory. Hard paste.
Painted blue, incised. 1744-1820. (h-i) VIENNA, Austria. Royal
Vienna, factory. Hard paste. Painted blue. 1750-1780.

j   k   l   m   n   o

(j) GERMANY. C. M. Hutschendreuther. Underglaze blue. Est.
1814. (k) VIENNA, Austria. Royal Vienna, factory. Hard paste.
1850-1864. (l) ANSBACH, Germany. Hard paste. Est. 1758. (m)
GERMANY. C. M. Hutschendreuther. Underglaze blue. Est. 1814.
(n) MALTA. Pottery. Impressed. 19th century. (o) LUDWIGS-
BURG, Germany. Porcelain. Est. 1756.

(**a**) NYMPHENBURG, Germany. Porcelain. Painted. 1800. (**b**)
NYMPHENBURG, Germany. Porcelain. Painted. 1754-1862. (**c**)
FRANKENTHAL, Germany. Porcelain. Painted blue. 1756. (**d**)
NYMPHENBURG, Germany. Porcelain. Painted. 1800. (**e**) GER-
MANY. Fayence. Circa 1830. (**f**) MEISSEN, Germany. Bottger
stoneware. 1724.

(**g**) MEISSEN, Germany. Bottger stoneware. 1710. (**h-i**) NUREM-
BERG, Germany. Fayence. Est. 1712. (**j**) SAVONA, Italy. Fayence.
17th century. (**k-l**) HEREND, Hungary. Moritz Fischer, owner.
Overglaze blue. 19th-20th century.

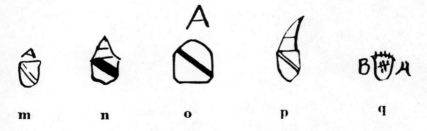

(**m-n-o-p**) ANSBACH, Germany. Hard paste. Painted blue. Est.
1758. (**q**) SAVONA, Italy. Fayence. 18th century.

a   b   c

(**a**) SAVONA, Italy. 18th century. (**b-c**) KLOSTER VEILSDORF, Germany. Porcelain. Underglaze blue. 1765.

d   e   f   g

(**d**) KLOSTER VEILSDORF, Germany. Porcelain. Underglaze blue. 1765. (**e**) WHEELING, West Virginia, U.S.A. Ohio Valley China Company. 1890. (**f**) SAVONA, Italy. Fayence. 18th century. (**g**) ALT-ROHLAU, Germany. Pottery, porcelain. Est. 1813.

h   i   j   k   l

(**h**) STEUBENVILLE, Ohio, U.S.A. Steubenville Pottery Company. Est. 1887. (**i**) EAST LIVERPOOL, Ohio, U.S.A. Burford Brothers Pottery Company. Circa 1880. (**j**) TRENTON, New Jersey, U.S.A. Crescent Pottery Company. Est. 1881. (**k**) LONGPORT, Great Britain. John Davenport, potter. Earthenware, porcelain. Printed. Circa 1800. (**l**) SEVRES, France. Mark tells year of decoration. 1902-1940.

a   b   c   d

(a) STEUBENVILLE, Ohio, U.S.A. Steubenville Pottery Company. Est. 1887. (b) SEVRES, France. Mark tells year of gilding. 1902-1940. (c) FENTON, Great Britain. Circa 1830. (d) SHELTON, Great Britain. 1815.

e   f   g   h   i

(e) MIDDLESBOROUGH, Great Britain. Earthenware. Impressed. 1845. (f) WORCESTER, Great Britain. Kerr and Binns. 1852-1862. (g) SCHLAGGENWALD, Germany. Lippert and Haas. 1832-1846. (h) LIMOGES, France. Haviland, factory. Whiteware. Painted green. 1936-1945. (i) TRENTON, New Jersey, U.S.A. Crescent Pottery Company. Est. 1881.

j   k   l   m   n

(j-k) BOSTON, Massachusetts, U.S.A. New England Pottery Company. Est. 1875. (l) TRENTON, New Jersey, U.S.A. Columbian Art Pottery Company. Est. 1876. (m) DOYLESTOWN, Pennsylvania, U.S.A. Moravian Pottery and Tile Works. Circa 1890. (n) GERMANY. Est. 1870.

a   b   c   d   e

(**a**) PIRKENHAMMER, Germany. Hard paste. Est. 1807. (**b**) WORCESTER, Great Britain. Kerr and Binns. Porcelain. 1852-1862. (**c**) GERMANY. Circa 1850. (**d**) BALTIMORE, Maryland, U.S.A. F. Haynes and Company. Est. 1880. (**e**) BALTIMORE, Maryland, U.S.A. Edwin Bennett. Circa 1875.

f   g   h   i   j

(**f**) TRENTON, New Jersey, U.S.A. Crescent Pottery Company. Est. 1881. (**g**) AKRON, Ohio, U.S.A. Summit China Company. Printed. Circa 1890. (**h**) KAOLIN, South Carolina, U.S.A. Southern Porcelain Company. Circa 1860. (**i**) HANLEY, Great Britain. Old Hall Porcelain Works. 20th century. (**j**) TONNOWA, Germany. Fayence, porcelain. 1813-1880.

k   l   m   n   o

(**k**) CHURCH GRESLEY, Great Britain. Porcelain. 1794-1808. (**l**) VOISONLIEU, France. Fayence. Impressed. 1839-1858. (**m-n**) METTLACH, Germany. Glazed earthenware. Est. 1809. (**o**) EAST HAMPTON, New York, U.S.A. Middle Lane Pottery. Circa 1890.

a   b   c   d   e

(**a**) BLOIS, France. Fayence. 19th century. (**b**) SHELTON, Great Britain. Brown-Westhead Moore and Company. Circa 1860. (**c**) CARLSBAD, Germany. Porcelain, earthenware. Est. 1803. (**d**) TRENTON, New Jersey, U.S.A. City Pottery Company. Circa 1860. (**e**) DERRY STATION, Pennsylvania, U.S.A. Derry China Company. 19th century.

f   g   h   i

(**f**) LAMBETH, Great Britain. Doulton, factory. After 1891. (**g**) EAST LIVERPOOL, Ohio, U.S.A. Potters Cooperative Company. Est. 1876. (**h**) BURSLEM, Great Britain. Earthenware. 19th century. (**i**) LIMOGES, France. Porcelain. After 1891.

j   k   l   m   n

(**j**) NYMPHENBURG, Germany. Johannes Klein, painter. Porcelain. 1765-1771. (**k**) TRENTON, New Jersey, U.S.A. Maddock Pottery Company. Circa 1900. (**l**) NOTTINGHAM, Great Britain. After 1891. (**m**) TUNSTALL, Great Britain. Pitcairns Limited. After 1891. (**n**) TRENTON, New Jersey, U.S.A. Prospect Hill Pottery Company. Est. 1880.

a   b   c   d

(a) LONGTON, Great Britain. Bridgwood and Son. 19th century.
(b) METTLACH, Germany. Earthenware. Est. 1809. (c-d) WOR-
CESTER, Great Britain. Grainger and Company. 1889.

e   f   g   h   i

(e) GOTHA, Germany. Porcelain. After 1830. (f) EAST LIVER-
POOL, Ohio, U.S.A. D. E. McNichal Pottery Company. After 1892.
(g) COBRIDGE, Great Britain. Henry Alcock and Company. 19th
century. (h) EAST LIVERPOOL, Ohio, U.S.A. East Liverpool Pottery Company. Circa 1900. (i) METTLACH, Germany. Earthenware. Est. 1809.

j   k   l   m   n

(j) BURSLEM, Great Britain. Wood and Barker. 19th century.
(k) WITTENBERGER, Germany. Est. 1884. (l) LIMOGES,
France. Porcelain. After 1891. (m-n) LAMBETH, Great Britain.
Doulton, factory. After 1891.

a   b   c   d   e

(**a**) TRENTON, New Jersey, U.S.A. Greenwood Pottery Company. Printed. Est. 1864. (**b**) LIVERPOOL, Ohio, U.S.A. Knowles, Taylor, and Knowles. Est. 1854. (**c**) BOSTON, Massachusetts, U.S.A. New England Pottery Company. Printed. Est. 1875. (**d**) WELLSVILLE, Ohio, U.S.A. Pioneer Pottery Company. Circa 1890. (**e**) TRENTON, New Jersey, U.S.A. Coxon and Company. Circa 1875.

f   g   h   i   j

(**f**) LIVERPOOL, Ohio, U.S.A. Knowles, Taylor, and Knowles. Est. 1854. (**g**) TORONTO, Ohio, U.S.A. American China Company. Est. 1896. (**h**) HANLEY, Great Britain. Fayence. F. Winkle and Company. 19th century. (**i**) TRENTON, New Jersey. U.S.A. Fell and Thropp Company. 19th century. (**j**) TRENTON, New Jersey, U.S.A. Greenwood Pottery Company. Porcelain. Printed. 1880.

k   l   m   n   o

(**k**) TRENTON, New Jersey, U.S.A. Crescent Pottery Company. Est. 1881. (**l**) BALTIMORE, Maryland, U.S.A. D. F. Haynes and Company. Est. 1879. (**m**) TRENTON, New Jersey, U.S.A. East Trenton Pottery Company. Circa 1890. (**n**) FENTON, Great Britain. John Edwards. After 1891. (**o**) TRENTON, New Jersey, U.S.A. Trenton Pottery Company. 19th century.

a   **b**   c   **d**

(**a**) WHEELING, West Virginia, U.S.A. Warwick China Company. Est. 1887. (**b-c**) EAST LIVERPOOL, Ohio, U.S.A. Knowles, Taylor, and Knowles. Est. 1854. (**d**) SAINT PETERSBURG, Russia. After 1830.

e   **f**   **g**   **h**

(**e**) SYRACUSE, New York, U.S.A. Onondaga Pottery Company. Est. 1871. (**f**) ZELL, Germany. Glazed earthenware. Est. 1818. (**g**) GERMANY. Circa 1875. (**h**) BURSLEM, Great Britain. Enoch Wood and Sons. 1818-1846.

i   j   k

(**i**) METTLACH, Germany. Fayence. 1842. (**j**) ZELL. Germany. Glazed earthenware. After 1818. (**k**) STOKE-ON-TRENT, Great Britain. Porcelain. Printed. Circa 1799.

a   b   c

(a) SCHLAGGENWALD, Germany. Porcelain. 1793-1866. (b) STOKE-ON-TRENT, Great Britain. Spode, factory. Copeland and Garrett. 1833-1847. (c) · BENNINGTON, Vermont, ·U.S.A. Impressed. Circa 1850.

d   e   f

(d) LONGPORT, Great Britain. G. Phillps, potter. Earthenware. 19th century. (e) STOKE-ON-TRENT, Great Britain. Minton, factory. After 1868. (f) SHELTON, Great Britain. Porcelain. 19th century.

g   h   i

(g) STOKE-ON-TRENT, Great Britain. Minton, factory. 1850. (h) COBRIDGE, Great Britain. Circa 1850. (i) STOKE-ON-TRENT, Great Britain. Spode, factory. 19th century.

SECTION **SQUARE**
See also Sections
**Circle and Sign,
Shield**

a   b   c   d   e

(**a-b**) MEISSEN, Germany. Bottger red stoneware. 1710-20. (**c**)
NEWCASTLE, Great Britain. John and David Elers, potters. Stoneware. 1690-1710. (**d**) CHELSEA, Great Britain. Porcelain. 1745-
1785. (**e**) HOLLAND. De Porceleyne Byl (The Porcelain Hatchet).
Fayence. Delft. 1759.

f   g   h   i   j

(**f**) WORCESTER, Great Britain. Porcelain. Blue underglaze. Est.
1751. (**g-h**) MEISSEN, Germany. Bottger red stoneware. Circa
1718. (**i-j**) WORCESTER, Great Britain. Porcelain. Est. 1751.

k   l   m   n   o

(**k-l-m**) WORCESTER, Great Britain. Porcelain. Blue Underglaze.
Est. 1751. (**n**) DERBY, Great Britain. Painted blue. 1775. (**o**)
WORCESTER, Great Britain. Porcelain. Blue underglaze. Est. 1751.

a b c d e

(**a**) WORCESTER, Great Britain. Porcelain. Blue underglaze. Est. 1751. (**b**) TUNSTALL, Great Britain. William Adams, potter. 1787-1805. (**c**) BOW, Great Britain. Est. 1750. (**d**) HANLEY, Great Britain. Impressed. Circa 1875. (**e**) STOKE-ON-TRENT, Great Britain. Spode, factory. Copeland, late Spode. Printed blue. 1847-1891.

f g h i

E. BRAIN & CO., LTD.

(**f**) DEDHAM, Massachusetts, U.S.A. Dedham Pottery Company. Circa 1900. (**g**) BOW, Great Britain. Est. 1750. (**h**) PARIS, France. 1773. (**i**) STOKE-ON-TRENT, Great Britain. E. Brain and Company Limited. Foley China Company. 20th century.

j k l m

(**j**) FRANCE. Hard paste. 1860. (**k**) SHELTON, Great Britain. 1762. (**l**) TRENTON, New Jersey, U.S.A. William Young and Sons. Circa 1855. (**m**) PRAGUE, Germany. Kriegel and Company. Porcelain. 1836-1862.

a   b   c   d   e

(**a**) LONGTON, Great Britain. Mayer and Newbold, potters. Painted red. 19th century. (**b**) NEWBURYPORT, Massachusetts, U.S.A. Merrimac Ceramic Company. Est. 1897. (**c**) FENTON, Great Britain. 18th century. (**d**) NEW ORLEANS, Louisiana, U.S.A. Newcomb Pottery Company. 19th century. (**e**) SEVRES, France. Painted black on hard paste, blue on soft paste. 1912-1917, 1921-1927.

f   g   h   i   j

(**f-g**) STOKE-ON-TRENT, Great Britain. Spode, factory. Ironstone. Printed blue. 1847-1891. (**h**) NEW YORK, New York, U.S.A. Carr and Morrison. 1853-1888. (**i**) WORCESTER, Great Britain. Porcelain. Painted color. Est. 1751. (**j**) ZELL, Germany. Glazed earthenware. After 1818.

k   l   m.   n   o

(**k**) HOLLAND. Fayence. Delft. 1705. (**l**) COLORADO SPRINGS, Colorado, U.S.A. Van Briggle Pottery Company. Est. 1900. (**m**) STOKE-ON-TRENT, Great Britain. After 1891. (**n**) STEUBENVILLE, Ohio, U.S.A. Steubenville Pottery Company. Est. 1887. (**o**) LONGTON, Great Britain. Hilditch and Son. Est. 1830.

$$\boxed{\text{MEIGH}}$$

$$\boxed{\text{MEISSEN}}$$

$$\boxed{\text{MYATT}}$$

a   b   c

(**a**) HANLEY, Great Britain. Job Meigh, potter. 18th century. (**b**) MEISSEN, Germany. Impressed. 19th century. (**c**) FENTON, Great Britain. Myatt, potter. Staffordshire. Impressed. 18th-19th century.

d   e   f   g   h

(**d**) NIDERVILLER, France. Fayence. Impressed. 1780-1800. (**e**) NEW YORK, New York, U.S.A. Carr and Morrison. Printed. 1855-1871. (**f**) EAST LIVERPOOL, Ohio, U.S.A. William Brunt Pottery Company. 1850-1895. (**g**) PRAGUE, Germany. Porcelain. 1810-1862. (**h**) GERMANY. 1820.

i   j   k   l

(**i**) NEW YORK, New York, U.S.A. Carr and Morrison. Printed. 1855-1871. (**j**) STOKE-ON-TRENT. Great Britain. Spode, factory. 1845-1891. (**k**) LUNEVILLE, France. Fayence. Circa 1775. (**l**) LIMOGES, France. Porcelain. 19th century.

a　　　　　　b　　　　　c　　　　　d

(a) METUCHEN, New Jersey, U.S.A. Charles Volkmar and Son.
Est. 1903. (b-c) CHODAU, Germany. Est. 1804. (d) SCHLAG-
GENWALD, Germany. Porcelain. 1793-1866.

f　　　　　　　　　g

(e) ALT-ROHLAU, Germany. 1813. (f) SHELTON, Great Britain.
John and William Ridgway. 1802. (g) BURSLEM, Great Britain.
Doulton, factory. After 1891.

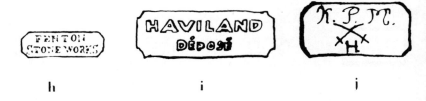

h　　　　　　　　i　　　　　　　　j

(h) FENTON, Great Britain. Staffordshire. 1800. (i) HAVILAND,
France. Whiteware. 1856. (j) MEISSEN, Germany. Hard paste.
1723.

a   b   c   d   e

(a) ALT-ROHLAU, Germany. Porcelain, fayence. Est. 1814. (b) PHILADELPHIA, Pennsylvania, U.S.A. Richard Remmey (Remney). Impressed. Est. 1859. (c) SEVRES, France. Hard paste. 1849. (d) SEVRES, France. Painted green on hard paste, black on hard paste, blue on soft paste. 1848-1899. (e) SEVRES, France. Hard paste, undecorated when it left the factory. Printed green. 1861.

f   g   h   i

(f) SEVRES, France. Porcelain. 1860-1891. (g) SARREGUE-MINES, France. Utzchneider and Company. Fayence. 19th century. (h) BALTIMORE, Maryland, U.S.A. Edwin Bennett. Circa 1875. (i) BOSTON, Massachusetts, U.S.A. New England Pottery Company. Circa 1887.

j   k   l   m

(j) TRENTON, New Jersey, U.S.A. Glasgow Pottery Company. 1863-1890. (k) BALTIMORE, Maryland, U.S.A. Maryland Pottery Company. Est. 1879. (l) NEW MILFORD, Connecticut, U.S.A. New Milford Pottery Company. Est. 1887. (m) WHEELING, West Virginia, U.S.A. Ohio Valley China Company. Circa 1890.

a   b   c   d

(**a**) LONGTON, Great Britain. Poole and Unwin, potters. 19th century. (**b**) WHEELING, West Virginia, U.S.A. Wheeling Pottery Company. Est. 1879. (**c**) BALTIMORE, Maryland, U.S.A. Edwin Bennett. 1856. (**d**) BEAVER FALLS, Pennsylvania, U.S.A. Mayer Pottery Company. Est. 1881.

e   f   g   h   i

(**e**) GREAT BRITAIN, 1842-1867 (see Foreword for complete explanation). (**f**) GREAT BRITAIN. 1868-1883 (see Foreword for complete explanation). (**g**) SEVRES, France. Painted black on hard paste, blue on soft paste. 1912-1917, 1921-1927. (**h**) PHILADELPHIA, Pennsylvania, U.S.A. J. E. Jeffords and Company. Printed. Circa 1875. (**i**) U.S.A. William Bloor. Impressed. 1862.

j   k   l   m

(**j**) COLORADO SPRINGS, Colorado, U.S.A. Van Briggle Pottery Company. Est. 1901. (**k**) BALTIMORE, Maryland, U.S.A. F. Haynes and Company. 1882-1884. (**l**) PHOENIXVILLE, Pennsylvania, U.S.A. Chester Pottery Company. Est. 1894. (**m**) LUNEVILLE, France. Fayence. Circa 1775.

a   b   c   d   e

(**a**) EAST LIVERPOOL, Ohio, U.S.A. Vodrey Brothers. Circa
1875. (**b**) PENNSYLVANIA, U.S.A. Pennsylvania Museum and
School of Industrial Art. Est. 1903. (**c**) NEW YORK, New York,
U.S.A. Union Porcelain Works. Circa 1880. (**d**) WHEELING, West
Virginia, U.S.A. Wheeling Pottery Company. Est. 1879. (**e**)
BEAVER FALLS, Pennsylvania, U.S.A. Mayer Pottery Company.
Est. 1881.

f   g   h   i

(**f**) STEUBENVILLE, Ohio, U.S.A. Steubenville Pottery Company.
Est. 1887. (**g**) EAST LIVERPOOL, Ohio, U.S.A. Knowles, Taylor,
and Knowles. Est. 1854. (**h**) GERMANY. Circa 1835. (**i**) EAST
LIVERPOOL, Ohio, U.S.A. Brunt, Bloor, and Martin. Est. 1876.

j   k   l   m

(**j**) EAST LIVERPOOL, Ohio, U.S.A. Knowles, Taylor, and
Knowles. Est. 1854. (**k**) FLEMINGTON, New Jersey, U.S.A. Ful-
per Brothers. Impressed. 19th century. (**l**) EAST LIVERPOOL,
Ohio, U.S.A. Knowles, Taylor, and Knowles. Est. 1854. (**m**)
DERBY, Great Britain. Robert Bloor. 1811-1848.

a   b   c   d   e

(**a**) SWANSEA, Wales. Porcelain. 1814-1822. (**b**) EAST LIVER-
POOL, Ohio, U.S.A. Brunt, Bloor, and Martin. Est. 1876. (**c**) FLEM-
INGTON, New Jersey, U.S.A. Fulper Brothers. Impressed. 19th
century. (**d**) BALTIMORE, Maryland, U.S.A. F. Haynes and Com-
pany. 1880-1890. (**e**) EAST LIVERPOOL, Ohio, U.S.A. Knowles,
Taylor, and Knowles. Est. 1854.

f   g   h   i

(**f**) SHELTON, Great Britain. John Ridgway, potter. Staffordshire.
After 1802. (**g**) LIMOGES, France. Porcelain. After 1891. (**h**)
FLEMINGTON, New Jersey, U.S.A. Impressed. 19th century. (**i**)
EAST LIVERPOOL, Ohio, U.S.A. Brunt, Bloor, and Martin. Est.
1876.

j   k   l   m

(**j**) EAST LIVERPOOL, Ohio, U.S.A. Knowles, Taylor, and
Knowles. Est. 1876. (**k**) BURSLEM, Great Britain. Moseley, potter.
Staffordshire. 1811-1857. (**l**) NEWCASTLE-ON-TYNE, Great Britain. Earthenware. 18th-19th century. (**m**) BEAVER FALLS, Pennsylvania, U.S.A. Mayer Pottery Company. Est. 1881.

a   **b**   **c**   **d**

(**a**) FENTON, Great Britain. Joseph Myatt. 18th-19th century. (**b**) EAST PALESTINE, Ohio, U.S.A. Ohio China Company. 19th century. (**c**) FLEMINGTON, New Jersey, U.S.A. Fulper Brothers. Impressed. 19th century. (**d**) BEAVER FALLS, Pennsylvania, U.S.A. Mayer Pottery Company. Est. 1881.

e   **f**   **g**   **h**

(**e**) BURSLEM, Great Britain. John and Richard Riley, potters. Staffordshire. 19th century. (**f-g**) CINCINNATI, Ohio, U.S.A. Rookwood Pottery Company. Circa 1880. (**h**) BURSLEM, Great Britain. Ralph Salt, potter. Impressed. 19th century.

i   **j**   **k**   **l**

(**i**) WELLSVILLE, Ohio, U.S.A. Wellsville China Company. Est. 1879. (**j**) EAST LIVERPOOL, Ohio, U.S.A. Union Potteries Company. 19th century. (**k**) STOKE-ON-TRENT, Great Britain. W. T. Copeland and Sons. Spode, factory. 1847-1891. (**l**) EAST LIVERPOOL, Ohio, U.S.A. Knowles, Taylor, and Knowles. Est. 1876.

a   b   c   d

(a) EAST LIVERPOOL, Ohio, U.S.A. Knowles, Taylor, and
Knowles. Est. 1854. (b) FLEMINGTON, New Jersey, U.S.A. Ful-
per Brothers. Impressed. 19th century. (c-d) BEAVER FALLS,
Pennsylvania, U.S.A. Mayer Pottery Company. Est. 1881.

e   f   g

(e) LISBON, Ohio, U.S.A. Thomas China Company. 19th century.
(f) BENNINGTON, Vermont, U.S.A. United States Pottery Company. Porcelain. Circa 1850. (g) STEUBENVILLE, Ohio, U.S.A.
Steubenville Pottery Company, Est. 1887.

h   i   j   k

(h) BURSLEM, Great Britain. John Walton. Earthenware. 18th-
19th century. (i) WELLSVILLE, Ohio, U.S.A. Pioneer Pottery
Company. Circa 1890. (j) EAST LIVERPOOL, Ohio, U.S.A. Vodrey Brothers. Circa 1875. (k) EAST LIVERPOOL, Ohio, U.S.A.
Brunt, Bloor, and Martin. Est. 1876.

SECTION **STAR
AND SUN**
See also Section
Lines

a   b   c   d   e

(**a**) DERBY, Great Britain. Isaac Farnsworth. 18th-19th century.
(**b**) GINORI, Italy. 1737. (**c**) THURINGIA, Germany. Wallendorf,
factory. Porcelain. 1764. (**d**) HOLLAND. De Ster (The Star).
Fayence. Delft. 1690. (**e**) BARANOVKA, Russia. Porcelain. Circa
1805.

f   g   h   i   j

(**f-g-h**) DOCCIA, Italy. Ginori, factory. Soft paste. Painted color.
1735. (**i**) CAUGHLEY, Great Britain. Porcelain. 1750. (**j**) HOL-
LAND. De Ster (The Star). Fayence. Delft. 1759.

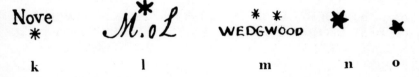

k   l   m   n   o

(**k**) NOVE, Italy. Fayence, porcelain. Painted gold, color. Est. 1728.
(**l**) OUDE LOOSDRECHT, Holland. Porcelain. Painted blue, red.
1771. (**m**) ETRURIA, Great Britain. Wedgwood, factory. Impressed. 1765-1850. (**n**) NOVE, Italy. Hard paste. Painted gold,
color. Est. 1728. (**o**) DOCCIA, Italy. Ginori, factory. 18th century.

(**a**) TRENTON, New Jersey, U.S.A. Star Porcelain Company. 19th century. (**b**) DOCCIA, Italy. Soft paste. Painted gold. 1735. (**c**) NYMPHENBURG, Germany. Hard paste. Est. 1755. (**d**) MIS-KOLEZ, Germany. Est. 1882. (**e**) FAENZA, Italy. Circa 1880.

(**f**) SAVONA, Italy. 18th century. (**g**) SEVILLE, Spain. 19th century. (**h**) HOLLAND. De Ster (The Star). Fayence. Delft. 1720. (**i**) EAST LIVERPOOL, Ohio, U.S.A. Globe Pottery Company. Est. 1888. (**j**) WELLSVILLE, Ohio, U.S.A. Wellsville China Company. Est. 1879.

(**k**) EAST LIVERPOOL, Ohio, U.S.A. C. C. Thompson Pottery Company. Est. 1888. (**l**) TRENTON, New Jersey, U.S.A. Trenton Pottery Company. Est. 1865. (**m**) NEVERS, France. Fayence. 17th century. (**n-o**) NEW CUMBERLAND. West Virginia, U.S.A. Chelsea China Company. Printed. Est. 1888.

a   b   c   d   e

(**a-b**) HOCHST, Germany. Hard paste. Painted blue, red, gold. 1750. (**c**) BALTIMORE, Maryland, U.S.A. Edwin Bennett. Circa 1875. (**d-e**) SAINT CLOUD, France. Soft paste. Painted blue. 1678-1766.

f   g   h   i   j

(**f**) DERBY, Great Britain. Robert Bloor. 1811-1848. (**g-h**) NEW MILFORD, Connecticut, U.S.A. Milford Pottery Company. Est. 1886. (**i-j**) HORNBERG, Germany. Horn Brothers. Fayence. 1880.

SECTION **TOWER**
See also Section
Miscellaneous

k   l   m   n   o

(**k**) WURZBURG, Germany. Hard paste. Painted blue. 1775. (**l**) CINCINNATI, Ohio, U.S.A. Rookwood Pottery Company. Circa 1880. (**m**) VINCENNES, France. Soft paste. Painted color, 1753. (**n**) LA TOUR D'AIGUES, France. Fayence. Est. 1753 (may be Tournay mark). (**o**) TOURNAY, Belgium. Soft paste. Est. 1751.

a   b   c   d   e

(**a**) LA TOUR D'AIGUES, France. Fayence. Est. 1753 (may be Tournay mark). (**b**) TOURNAY, Belgium. Soft paste. Est. 1751. (**c**) CLIGNANCOURT, France. Hard paste. Painted blue, gold. 1771-1798. (**d**) SAVONA, Italy. 18th century. (**e**) GERMANY. Circa 1840.

f   g   h   i   j

(**f**) FLORENCE, Italy. Soft paste. Painted color. 1580. (**g**) GERMANY. Circa 1840. (**h**) TOURNAY, Belgium. Soft paste. Est. 1751. (**i**) LIEGE, Belgium. Fayence. 1752-1811. (**j**) WHEELING, West Virginia, U.S.A. Wheeling Pottery Company. Est. 1903.

k   l   m

(**k**) COPENHAGEN, Denmark. Bing and Grondahl, factory. 1853. (**l**) BURSLEM, Great Britain. 1795. (**m**) METTLACH, Germany. Glazed earthenware. Est. 1809.

a   b   c

(a) HAVILAND, France. Whiteware. Painted green. 1892. (b) OLD HALL, Great Britain. Earthenware. 19th century. (c) GERMANY. Zsolnay. Soft paste. Est. 1855.

d   e   f   g   h   i

SECTION
TRIANGLE AND HEART
See also Sections
Circle and Sign, Shield

(d) CHELSEA, Great Britain. Soft paste. Painted gold, red. 1745-1750. (e) BOW, Great Britain. Incised, painted blue, red. Est. 1750. (f) DERBY, Great Britain. Hard paste. Painted blue, impressed. Est. 1745. (g) CHELSEA, Great Britain. Soft paste. 1745-1750. (h) BOW, Great Britain. Porcelain. Incised. Est. 1750. (i) KORZEC, Poland. Porcelain. 1790-1797.

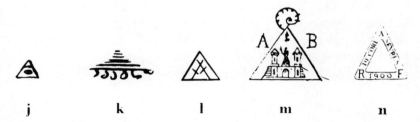

j   k   l   m   n

(j) KORZEC, Poland. Porcelain. 1790-1797. (k) PERSIA. 19th century. (l) BRISTOL, Great Britain. Hard paste. Impressed. 18th century. (m) MAGDEBURG, Germany. 1799-1865. (n) SEVRES, France. Mark tells year of decoration. 1900-1902.

a   b   c   d

(**a**) SEVRES, France. Painted red. Guilder's mark. 1900-1902. (**b**) QUIMPER, France. Fayence. 1782-1872. (**c**) MEISSEN, Germany. Porcelain. Impressed. 1766-1780. (**d**) KORZEC, Poland. Porcelain. 1790-1797.

e   f   g   h   i

(**e**) STEUBENVILLE, Ohio, U.S.A. Lonhuda Pottery Company. Est. 1892. (**f**) BURSLEM, Great Britain. 19th century. (**g**) SEVRES, France. Hard paste painted black, soft paste painted blue. 1900-1911. (**h**) GERMANY. Est. 1889. (**i**) SARREGUIMINES, France. Porcelain, fayence. 19th century.

j   k   l   m

(**j**) HANLEY, Great Britain. 19th century. (**k**) NEWCASTLE, Great Britain. 19th century. (**l-m**) ORLEANS, France. Hard paste, soft paste. Painted color. 1753-1812.

a   b   c   d

(**a**) TOURNAY, Belgium. Est. 1753. (**b**) BRUGES, Belgium. 18th century. (**c**) PARIS, France. Rue Popincourt, factory. Porcelain. 1782-1835. (**d**) Liverpool, Great Britain. Richard Chaffers. 1740-1765.

e   f   g   h

(**e**) MOUSTIERS, France. Fayence. Painted color. 17th century. (**f**) NAPLES, Italy. Painted color. 16th century. (**g**) FRANCE. Fayence. Impressed. Circa 1830. (**h**) MILAN, Italy. Fayence. 18th century.

i   j   k

(**i**) GERMANY. Fayence. 19th century. (**j**) GERMANY. Benedikt Brothers. Est. 1884. (**k**) LIVERPOOL, Great Britain. Richard Chaffers. 1740-1765.

INDEX OF MARKS

INDEX OF MANUFACTURERS